Bernice Lee

The Security Implications of the New Taiwan

Adelphi Paper 331

Oxford University Press, Great Clarendon Street, Oxford OX2 6DP
Oxford New York
Athens Auckland Bangkok Bombay Calcutta Cape Town
Dar es Salaam Delhi Florence Hong Kong Istanbul Karachi
Kuala Lumpur Madras Madrid Melbourne Mexico City
Nairobi Paris Singapore Taipei Tokyo Toronto
and associated companies in
Berlin Ibadan

Oxford is a trade mark of Oxford University Press

Published in the United States
by Oxford University Press Inc., New York

© The International Institute for Strategic Studies 1999

First published October 1999 by **Oxford University Press** for
The International Institute for Strategic Studies
23 Tavistock Street, London WC2E 7NQ

Director John Chipman
Editor Gerald Segal
Assistant Editor Matthew Foley
Project Manager, Design and Production Mark Taylor

British Library Cataloguing in Publication Data
Data available

Library of Congress Cataloguing in Publication Data

ISBN 0-19-922479-X
ISSN 0567-932x

contents

map & tables

glossary

ADB	Asian Development Bank
APEC	Asia-Pacific Economic Cooperation
ARATS	Association for Relations Across the Taiwan Straits (China)
ASEAN	Association of South-East Asian Nations
CCP	Chinese Communist Party
DPP	Democratic Progressive Party (Taiwan)
GIO	Government Information Office (Taiwan)
GNP	gross national product
KMT	Kuomintang
MAC	Mainland Affairs Council (Taiwan)
MEA	Ministry of Economic Affairs (Taiwan)
MFA	Ministry of Foreign Affairs (China)
MFN	Most Favored Nation
NDC	National Development Conference (Taiwan)
NPC	National People's Congress (China)
NUC	National Unification Council (Taiwan)
PLA	People's Liberation Army
PRC	People's Republic of China
ROC	Republic of China
SAR	Special administrative region (China)
SEF	Straits Exchange Foundation (Taiwan)

Relations between China and Taiwan suffered their worst crisis for 40 years in 1995–96. In an attempt to influence the outcome of elections in Taiwan, China fired nuclear-capable missiles and held large-scale military exercises near the island. In response, the US sent two aircraft-carrier battle groups to the area, demonstrating its willingness to risk war with Beijing to defend the principle that force should not be used to settle the China–Taiwan dispute. The US deployments were the largest in Asia for 20 years. The crisis made it crystal clear, if there was ever any doubt, that relations between China and Taiwan are not only about trade, investment and tourism, but also about war and peace.

The crisis ended with an unspoken agreement to return to the ambiguities that had for many years kept the peace in the Taiwan Strait. This uneasy calm did not, however, last for long. On 9 July 1999, Taiwanese President Lee Teng-hui shattered it with the assertion that relations between China and Taiwan should be conducted on a 'special state-to-state basis'. Lee's new formulation, while carefully avoiding declaring Taiwan an independent state, threatened to explode the 'one-China' myth that had allowed the main actors to side-step the fact of Taiwan's growing separation from the mainland. By declaring that Taipei should be seen as an international actor on a par with Beijing, Lee was coming as close to declaring independence as was possible, without actually doing so.

Three major issues lie behind the dispute between Taiwan and China. The first, and by far the most important, is Taiwan's

Map I *China and Taiwan*

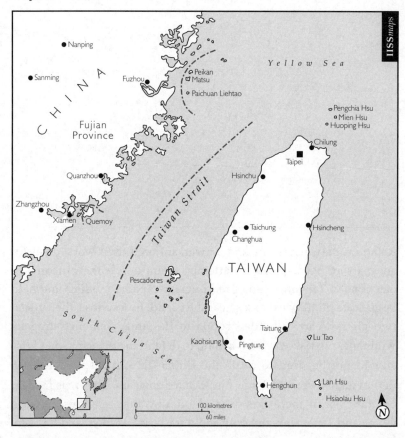

democratisation. As a new and more vocal middle class emerged from decades of economic growth, the island's autocratic system has, since the 1980s, given way to increasingly liberal politics. In turn, a new Taiwanese identity has taken shape, defining a more confident and independent-minded polity. The second issue – China's growing threat to retake Taiwan by force – is in many ways a response to these developments. As the island's self-confidence has grown, so too has a more assertive nationalism on the mainland. Faced with the risk that Taiwan might slip from their grasp, China's leaders chose intimidation through force in 1995–96. With Lee raising the stakes in 1999, the risk has grown that Beijing may see no alternative but to do so again. Indecisive US foreign policy towards the China–

Taiwan conflict is the third factor at work in the dispute. When the 1995–96 crisis broke, divisions between the US Congress and the president, together with incoherence in general US policy towards China, produced an uncertain and vague reaction. Although in the end the US military response was robust, without a coherent or firm policy, no one can be sure that it will be so again should cross-Strait relations face another crisis.

Increased economic links between Taiwan and China have not resolved the differences across the Strait, and all the parties concerned have difficult choices to make. On the one hand, the US is convinced of the need to ensure that Beijing does not use military means to settle the issue. On the other, it recognises that giving Taiwan's leaders *carte blanche* in their policy choices will guarantee that China will use force. For China, compromise on such a fundamental nationalist issue as Taiwan is inconceivable. But Beijing also knows that using force will threaten its economic-modern-isation programme by alarming its neighbours and the international business community, so vital to reform. Taiwan's progress towards a new identity and greater self-determination seems unstoppable, but the island's politicians remain unsure as to how gingerly they should approach their goal. Without careful management of these issues, there is a serious risk of conflict threatening not only Asian, but also global, security.

chapter 1

The History of the Relationship

Early History

The conflict between China and Taiwan is so deeply entwined with the competing claims of an ancient Chinese nationalism and a newly emerging Taiwanese identity that it is worthwhile stepping back, however briefly, to the absolute basics of the dispute. Taiwan lies about 160 kilometres off the south-east coast of mainland China. According to the 'official' Chinese version, the island's history began in 1430, when Cheng He, an explorer sent by Ming Emperor Hsuan Tsung, landed there. However, records of contact between Taiwan and the mainland date back to the sixth century. Expansionist Sui Dynasty Emperor Yang-ti sent expeditions to the island to demand tribute from its aboriginal inhabitants. Taiwan is thought to have been home to two groups at this time. The first, the Proto-Malay, were part of the Southern Paleo-Mongoloid racial group which had migrated across South-east Asia from the Philippines, settling in southern Taiwan in the seventh century. The second, known as 'Lonkius' by the Japanese and 'Taiyals' and 'Vonums' by the Chinese, inhabited the north of the island. The origins of this group are disputed. Japanese ethnologists believe that the Lonkius were descended from the Ainu people of the northern Japanese island of Hokkaido; the Chinese, however, argue that they were mainlanders who emigrated from present-day Guizhou to Taiwan as early as 1700 BC.[1]

Towards the end of the twelfth century, fishermen from Taiwan began plundering villages in Fujian, and mainland Chinese started to set up trading posts and settlements on the island. Emigration gathered pace as the Sung Dynasty began to collapse in the second half of the thirteenth century. With the advent of the Yuan Dynasty in 1279, the Hakka people of Fujian and Guangdong began to cross the Strait, fleeing first the Mongol advance, and then persecution under the Yuan. After brief imperial interest following Cheng He's landfall in 1430, the island was left largely to its own devices as a centre for Japanese and Taiwanese pirates. The Dutch, who were granted a base at Macao in 1557, were the first to take Taiwan seriously, renaming it Ilha Formosa ('Beautiful Island') and ruling it as a colony between 1624 and 1662. Although Chinese historians have consistently underplayed the significance of the Dutch presence, it was important because it set Taiwan apart from the mainland.

Following the expulsion of the Dutch, Taiwan was ruled by the Cheng Cheng-Kung family until 1683, when the Qing Dynasty seized control, completing its conquest of all of China. Taiwan was incorporated into the Qing empire in 1683–84 as a prefecture and military district of Fujian province. A fresh wave of Han Chinese emigration followed. After its incorporation into the Qing empire, Taiwan was seen as a part of *'tienxia'* – 'all-under-heaven' – within the Sinocentric world-view which placed the Chinese Emperor, the Son of

China never really rules Taiwan

Heaven, at the apex of human society.[2] The main Chinese claim for sovereignty over Taiwan was based on the existence of historical records of Chinese missions to the island which predated those of other states. However, at the outset Taiwan was not regarded as a formal Chinese province, but as distant, uncivilised and rebellious – a career graveyard for Qing imperial officials.[3] Qing interest in Taiwan was confined to the rice and sugar that it produced.

Taiwan's military importance grew as the challenge to the Qing empire from the West and from Japan increased in the nineteenth century. In response to foreign encroachment on China's border regions, formal Qing rule was established on the island in 1874, and Taiwan became a formal province of China in 1885. Ten years later, however, the Japanese defeated Qing forces; Taiwan was ceded under the Treaty of Shimonoseki, becoming Japan's first colony. Taiwan's colonisation by Japan is one of the most important episodes in the island's history. Japan regarded the island as an imperial showcase and, despite anti-Japanese uprisings, the Taiwanese generally saw colonisation as an improvement on the bureaucratic inertia and neglect that had marked mainland rule. Inter-tribal rivalry declined markedly, the economy was modernised and industrialised and living standards improved.[4] By the end of the Second World War, many of the fundamentals of the Taiwanese economy were on a par with those of Japan.[5]

By the time Japan took control of Taiwan, Qing rule was on the verge of collapse. The final blow came in October 1911, when a military rebellion toppled the regime. In its place, the Republic of China (ROC) was established on 1 January 1912, with nationalist Sun Yat Sen as its president. Sun's leadership rapidly gave way to dictatorship under Yuan Shikai, who instituted a constitutional monarchy, made himself emperor and banned Sun's nationalist Kuomintang (KMT). Yuan's death in 1916 created a power vacuum, in which rival military commanders vied for control. Against this background of internal disunity and external weakness, the Chinese Communist Party (CCP) was founded in July 1921 in Shanghai. Three years later, Sun signed an accord with the Soviet Union, and reorganised the KMT along Leninist lines. Its organisational principle became 'democratic socialism', under which local cells owed obedience to directives from the centre. Encouraged by Moscow, the CCP cooperated with the KMT within a United Front.

The United Front was short-lived. Following Sun's death in March 1925, leadership of the KMT passed to Chiang Kai-shek, a soldier-turned-politician who shifted the party to the right, ended its links with Moscow and purged it of communists. By 1928, Chiang and the KMT were in effective control of most of China. However, factionalism, communist opposition and continued foreign encroachment meant that KMT rule on the mainland was never complete. In 1931, Japan invaded Manchuria and, by 1933, had extended its control to Inner Mongolia. In 1937, the KMT and the CCP, by then in control of north-west China, formed a second United Front to resist the occupation. Fighting between Chiang's forces and the CCP nonetheless continued.

In 1942, Chiang issued a formal claim to Taiwan. Although in draft constitutions in 1925, 1934 and 1936 the island had not been included as part of Chinese territory, Chiang changed his position in

1941, when the Allies made the recovery of Axis-occupied areas one of the major principles of the Atlantic Charter. Following Chiang's appearance at the Allied Cairo Conference on 1 December 1943, China's renewed claim to Taiwan gained international recognition.[6] When Japan surrendered on 25 October 1945, sovereignty over Taiwan returned to China. At the same time, the civil war between Chiang's KMT and Mao Zedong's CCP resumed in earnest. By 1949, communist victory on the mainland was imminent, and Chiang retreated to Taiwan. The People's Republic of China (PRC) was established on 1 October. Although the CCP rose to power as a Marxist–Leninist political party, it also had a significant nationalist element. Maintaining China's territorial integrity – including regaining control of Taiwan – was always a fundamental aim.

Although the US had backed the KMT against the communists during the civil war, President Harry Truman's administration had become increasingly disillusioned with its inefficiency and corruption, and US support did not immediately resume following the establishment of the PRC. This ambivalence vanished in 1950, when North Korea invaded the South, and Mao led China into the conflict on Pyongyang's side. In June 1950, the US Seventh Fleet deployed in the Taiwan Strait. During the Korean War, the US stepped up its supplies of arms and aid to Taiwan; between February 1950 and June 1954, aid was estimated at $1.4 billion. The Korean War consolidated the Cold War in Asia, freezing Sino-US relations for 20 years.[7] Washington imposed sanctions on China, froze Chinese assets in the US, embargoed trade and banned US ships and aircraft from calling at Chinese ports and airfields. US support for the KMT also meant that the Republic of China on Taiwan retained the China seat in the UN long after the consolidation of communist rule on the mainland, losing it only in October 1971.

Crises across the Strait

Following the Korean War armistice on 27 July 1953, Chinese attention turned to a number of islands in the Taiwan Strait under KMT jurisdiction, including Quemoy and Matsu. These islands were both advance bases for any attack against the mainland, and Taiwan's first line of defence. On 3 August 1954, US Secretary of State John Foster Dulles declared the offshore islands to be strategically linked to the protection of Taiwan, which had become an essential part of the 'island chain' of positions that the US was building across the Western Pacific. However, although negotiations over a mutual defence treaty between Taiwan and the US were under way, CCP leaders were unconvinced of Washington's willingness to defend Taiwan.

On 3 September 1954, Beijing tested the water by bombarding Quemoy, prompting Chiang to bomb the mainland in response. The following November, China attacked Ta Chen and other islands off the Fujian and Zhejiang coasts. By early 1955, Chinese forces had cut the supply routes to Taiwan and, on 5 February, KMT troops withdrew from Ta Chen with the help of the Seventh Fleet. China's actions sparked a heated debate in the US about Taiwan's defence, *China blows hot and cold* which concluded that many of its offshore islands could not be effectively protected because they were too close to the mainland. When the Mutual Defence Agreement was signed between the US and Taiwan in December 1954, only Taiwan and the Pescadores were specifically included.

At the height of the 1954–55 crisis, Beijing had made clear its intention to invade Taiwan. By mid-1955, however, the CCP had switched tactics. Deteriorating relations with the Soviet Union convinced China's leaders that they should avoid confrontation where possible. In a bid to ease tensions, China began negotiations with the US in August 1955. At the National People's Congress (NPC) the following year, Premier Zhou Enlai pledged that China would 'as far as possible' use peaceful means to 'liberate' Taiwan. However, with the start of the Great Leap Forward in 1957, talks between US and Chinese ambassadors were suspended and, in March 1958, the US State Department condemned the CCP regime as illegitimate. In turn, Beijing denounced US involvement in the Middle East as imperialist.

China's approach to Taiwan again became aggressive. Mao ordered the heavy bombing of Quemoy and Matsu on 23 August 1958, prompting fresh debate in Washington over the strategic significance of the islands. Between 24 and 30 August, the US built up its military presence, including an aircraft carrier, in the Taiwan Strait. President Dwight D. Eisenhower and Dulles announced that the US regarded the Strait, including Quemoy and Matsu, as being within its defence area. On 15 September 1958, talks opened between China and the US in Warsaw. In October, Beijing offered to negotiate a peaceful settlement with the nationalists, and announced that the PRC would suspend its bombardment. The crisis abated when US forces helped to break the Chinese blockade of the islands.

Changing Relations

Both Taiwan and China adjusted their strategies in the wake of the crisis. Taipei conceded that the offshore islands could not be used as a base from which to attack the mainland since any invasion would need US consent, which was unlikely. Beijing also questioned the islands' strategic importance, and recognised that occupying them might provoke confrontation with the US. The perceived failure of the Soviet Union to come to China's aid during the crisis meant that Beijing would probably face the US alone. China adopted a more conciliatory attitude in the 1960s, seeking to convince the Taiwanese that they were victims of US 'imperialism'. Officially, China maintained that it was ready to enter into negotiations with Taiwan to prepare for peaceful reunification, but would not renounce the use of force should it be deemed necessary.

Taiwan's official position remained consistent: no compromise and no contact with 'communist bandits'. A third of Taiwan's 400,000–500,000 troops were stationed on the offshore islands, and its navy and air force dominated the Taiwan Strait. Chiang periodically sought to capitalise on China's internal problems. In 1962, following the collapse of China's economy as a result of the Great Leap Forward, he planned to invade the mainland. He failed to enlist US support, and the idea came to nothing. In October 1967, during the turmoil of the Cultural Revolution, Chiang called for an anti-Mao alliance between the Taiwanese and Mao's communist opponents, again to no effect.

Towards the end of the 1960s, relations across the Strait changed. The Soviet invasion of Czechoslovakia in 1968, the Brezhnev Doctrine (outlining an assertive Soviet policy towards other communist states) and border clashes between Chinese and Soviet forces in March 1969 made closer relations with the US against the 'Soviet threat' more attractive in Beijing. Meanwhile, normalising relations with China would help the US to disentangle itself from Vietnam. National security adviser Henry Kissinger paid a secret visit to China on 9–11 July 1971 and, on 28 February 1972, both countries achieved a breakthrough in their relations when the Shanghai Communiqué was issued during a state visit by President Richard Nixon (see Appendix, page 71). However, in the communiqué, the US merely acknowledged that both Taipei and Beijing agreed that there was only one China. The US noted the PRC's claim to be the 'sole legal government' of China, but did not accept it. Japan and other major powers withdrew diplomatic recognition from Taiwan, and special arrangements were made for 'unofficial' representation in Taipei.

the US shifts position on Taiwan

It took several years for either Taiwan or China to develop a new strategy to deal with these changed circumstances. Chiang died in April 1975, and was succeeded by his 65-year-old son, Chiang Ching-kuo. Mao died the following year and, by 1978, it had become clear that Deng Xiaoping had succeeded in wresting power from Mao's anointed successor, Hua Guofeng. Deng, a reputed 'pragmatist', toned down China's hostile rhetoric in a bid to persuade the US formally to recognise the PRC. Recognition would facilitate US investment and make possible transfers of military technology, an important objective as Sino-Soviet relations deteriorated.

With the 'Joint Communiqué on the Establishment of Diplomatic Relations' of 1 January 1979, the US formally switched recognition from Taipei to Beijing (see Appendix, page 73). In the communiqué, the US acknowledged 'the Chinese position that there is but one China and Taiwan is part of China', while maintaining cultural, commercial and other unofficial relations with Taiwan. Washington declared that it retained an interest in 'the peaceful resolution of the Taiwan issue and expects [it] to be settled peacefully by the Chinese themselves'. Washington also gave a year's notice of the termination of the 1954 Mutual Defence Agreement. On 10 April, Congress responded to this perceived abandonment of Taiwan by passing the Taiwan Relations Act (TRA). Although the TRA fell short of the full commitment contained in the Mutual Defence Agreement, it did nonetheless provide the rationale for US intervention (see Appendix, page 74). Under the act, US policy was to:

*provide Taiwan with arms of a defensive character; and to
maintain the capacity of the United States to resist any resort
to force or other forms of coercion that would jeopardize the
security, or the social or economic system, of the people on
Taiwan.*

Following the 1979 communiqué, artillery exchanges between
Quemoy and Matsu and the mainland, which had long since
contained only propaganda leaflets, ceased. Military tensions across
the Strait appeared to ease significantly, and relations between China
and Taiwan entered a new phase. In December 1978, the CCP
decided on economic reform, including opening up the country to
the outside world. On 1 January 1979, the NPC issued a 'Message to
Compatriots on Taiwan', which called for cross-Strait talks, and for
the establishment of 'three links' – mail, transport and trade – and
'four exchanges' – economic, cultural, technical and sporting.
Threats were replaced by requests that the Taiwan issue be settled
peacefully. In September 1981, the chairman of the NPC's Standing
Committee, Marshal Ye Jianying, announced a nine-point proposal
'to bring an end to the unfortunate separation of the Chinese nation'
(see Appendix, page 76). The proposal called for talks and
exchanges, invited Taiwanese businesses to invest in mainland
enterprises and pledged that Taiwan's 'way of life and its economic
and cultural relations with foreign countries' would remain
unchanged after reunification. The island would continue to enjoy
autonomy, as well as its own defence capabilities.

Underlying Ye's proposal was the 'one country, two systems'
concept. In December 1982, the NPC adopted a new constitution,
which provided for special administrative regions (SARs) – the
status offered to Taiwan – with economic and political systems that
differed from those of the rest of the country. Deng also began
negotiations with the UK over the British colony of Hong Kong, and
with Portugal over Macao. In addition to this so-called 'smiling
diplomacy', Beijing launched a series of diplomatic offensives
designed to isolate Taiwan in the international community. States
around the world were warned that establishing official relations
with Taiwan would cost them their ties with China, and their access
to the emerging Chinese market.

Despite China's overtures, Taiwan continued to resist reunification and, in 1981, Taipei issued its so-called 'three noes': 'no negotiation', 'no contact' and 'no compromise with communism'. Nonetheless, both formal and informal relations across the Strait improved. This more pragmatic relationship with the mainland owed much to the liberalisation of Taiwan's domestic politics. Although formally illegal under martial law, the opposition Democratic Progressive Party (DPP) was formed in September 1986. Martial law was lifted in July 1987, and the KMT came under growing public pressure to ease control over

Taiwan becomes more pragmatic about China

civilian and economic contacts with China. In November 1987, restrictions on visits by Taiwanese residents to the mainland were officially lifted, and Taiwanese with two or more 'close' relatives on the mainland were permitted to travel there via a third country. Museum artefacts were exchanged, and a joint committee on the Mandarin language was established.

When Taiwanese Vice-President Lee Teng-hui became president following Chiang Ching-kuo's death in 1988, he formally changed the 'three noes' policy. A distinction was made between private, people-to-people contacts, which were to be encouraged, and official government ones, which remained prohibited.[8] In October 1990, Lee, by then an elected president, convened a consultative body, the National Unification Council (NUC), to advise on regulating the increasing flow of people and goods across the Strait. A Mainland Affairs Council (MAC) was established to direct cabinet-level planning, evaluation and coordination of policy. It was also responsible for some policy implementation. Although the MAC was officially under the Executive Yuan, the highest organ of the state, in practice it remained at the disposal of the Presidential Office. Council members included the heads of important ministries, as well as the chief of the security apparatus.[9] On 25 December 1990, Lee announced that the state of civil war with China (the 'Period of Mobilisation against Communist Rebellion') would end on 1 May 1991. Lee was rejecting the use of force to achieve unification, and was implicitly recognising the CCP as a political entity in effective control of the mainland. Lee's declaration also opened the way for official contacts. These could take place under a new formula: 'one-country, two governments', or 'one-China, two political entities'. These concepts, which were put forward by Taiwanese political leaders in the late 1980s, meant that Taiwan was regarded as historically a part of China, and should eventually be united with the mainland. In the meantime, however, the Taiwanese government should be viewed as legitimate.

Two further cross-Strait bodies were established in the early 1990s. Taiwan's Straits Exchange Foundation (SEF) was set up in November 1990 under the MAC to conduct unofficial contacts and negotiations with the mainland. Although formally unofficial, 80% of the SEF's funding is provided by the government, and the foundation works within guidelines set by the MAC. In November 1991, China established a counterpart organisation, the Association for Relations Across the Taiwan Straits (ARATS). While the SEF aimed to promote contacts and exchanges between China and Taiwan, ARATS was designed to encourage postal, trade, maritime and air links, and to 'carry out peaceful reunification ... on the basis of "one-country, two systems"'.[10]

Representatives from the SEF and ARATS met in Singapore on 27–29 April 1993. These negotiations were dubbed the Koo–Wang or Wang–Koo talks, after the head of the SEF delegation, Koo Chen Fu, a Taiwan-born industrialist, and the leader of the ARATS party, Wang Daohan, a former mayor of Shanghai. Koo was a KMT member and Lee confidant, while Wang was believed to have close ties with Chinese leader Jiang Zemin. Although symbolically significant, no agreement was reached on the agenda items, which included the repatriation of illegal immigrants and hijackers and fisheries disputes. Four agreements covering communications across the Strait were nonetheless signed.[11] Follow-up talks in November 1993 and March 1994 were inconclusive.

Trade, Investment and Economic Links

A key feature in the improved mood of cross-Strait relations was the potential for mutually beneficial economic links. Economic relations were made possible by Deng's 'open-door' strategy of 1978, which led to a dramatic increase in China's foreign trade. Between 1978 and 1991, China's merchandise trade grew by over 14% a year, almost double the growth-rate for global trade as a whole.[12]

Figure 1 *Trade across the Taiwan Strait, 1978–1998*

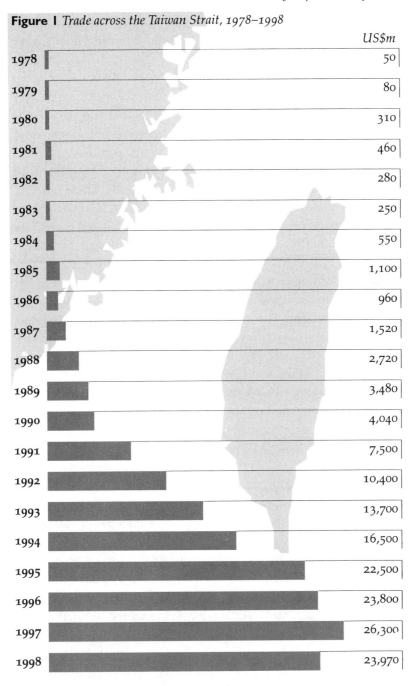

US$m

Year	US$m
1978	50
1979	80
1980	310
1981	460
1982	280
1983	250
1984	550
1985	1,100
1986	960
1987	1,520
1988	2,720
1989	3,480
1990	4,040
1991	7,500
1992	10,400
1993	13,700
1994	16,500
1995	22,500
1996	23,800
1997	26,300
1998	23,970

Note All figures are estimated

Sources Hong Kong Customs; Mainland Affairs Council; Straits Exchange Foundation

Trade levels between China and Taiwan fluctuated in the early 1980s. China initially waived tariffs on Taiwanese goods, gave them priority treatment and discounted sales to Taiwan by 20%. However, in response to an overheating economy and a growing trade deficit, China withdrew these preferential measures in May 1981, causing Taiwanese exports to decline in 1982 and 1983. Trade recovered following the reinstitution of preferential measures in April 1983. In September 1984, Beijing loosened controls on foreign exchange and imports. As a result, Taiwan's exports to the mainland rose by 111% in 1984, and by 132% in 1985.[13] In 1985, China formally opened its domestic market to Taiwanese investors, and designated ten coastal ports for Taiwanese investment, shipping and trade. Two years later, Beijing issued regulations to encourage Taiwanese investment by providing special tax incentives.

Establishing economic relations with China was regarded as fundamentally a political issue in Taiwan, and Taipei's response was initially lukewarm. The island's politicians suspected Beijing's motives, and sought to prevent its economy from becoming overly dependent on Chinese raw materials and labour. Taiwan's businesses, on the other hand, were keen to reduce the costs they incurred by having to use a third party to trade with, and invest in, China. Hong Kong, for example, was used by many Taiwanese firms as a point of re-export, imposing huge handling costs.[14] From the mid-1980s, rising land and labour costs in Taiwan prompted many of the island's businesses to relocate manufacturing plants to cheaper countries in the region, such as Malaysia and Vietnam. China's preferential tariff and tax arrangements, as well as linguistic and cultural affiliations, made it more attractive than South-east Asian states as an investment destination.

Taiwan officially lifted the embargo on indirect trade with China in July 1985. However, imports from China remained strictly regulated and, until the ban on visits to the mainland was removed in November 1987, no Taiwanese was allowed contact with mainland personnel or organisations. By May 1990, the list of mainland imports allowed via Hong Kong included just 155 categories of raw materials, all of which were also easily obtainable from other suppliers. Nonetheless, by the early 1990s Taiwan had become more amenable to cross-Strait trade and investment. In July 1990, the Ministry of Economic Affairs (MEA) passed a regulation governing indirect exports to the mainland, and another covering investment and technological cooperation. In 1993, the MEA allowed the import of 1,654 mainland products, a fifth of which were semi-finished. By the end of 1995, cumulative investment in China stood at an estimated $30bn – more than a third of Taiwan's total capital outflow, and greater than its investment in the whole of South-east Asia. Mainland China became Taiwan's second-largest export market after the US. According to Taiwanese statistics, the island's trade with the mainland in 1995 amounted to $22.5bn, or 17.4% of its total exports that year. In 1990, Taiwan's trade surplus with China was $7.04bn, out of an overall surplus of $12.5bn. By 1995, this had risen to $16.3bn, while its overall surplus had fallen to $8.12bn.[15] As economic interdependence grew, it began to appear that peaceful dialogue had replaced military conflict as the central feature of relations across the Strait. Events in 1995–96 would, however, shatter that illusion.

The Emergence of Taiwanese Democracy

Although the confrontation between China and Taiwan has important international aspects, domestic developments in both countries – notably democratisation in Taiwan – are the most significant agents of change. In the 1980s, a new generation of Taiwanese politicians emerged that did not share the 'one-China' vision traditionally held by both the KMT and the mainland regime. Authoritarian rule was relaxed, and a native Taiwanese nationalism began to take shape. Taiwan's economic success and the growth of the island's middle class fuelled demands for a more open political system, and for international recognition. These developments set the scene for a new phase of confrontation in the mid-1990s.

Political Reform

Following Japan's defeat in 1945, Chiang and the KMT retook Taiwan, and began to consolidate power. In the so-called '228 Incident' of 28 February 1947, the KMT brutally suppressed native Taiwanese activists. Between 5,000 and 10,000 people are thought to have been killed, resulting in decades of mistrust and hostility between 'mainlanders' and native Taiwanese. On 10 May 1948, the ROC's National Assembly granted Chiang unlimited powers under an emergency decree – 'The Temporary Provisions in Effect during the Period of Communist Rebellion' – establishing martial law.

When Chiang and the KMT fled to Taiwan in 1949, they brought with them 2.5m mainlanders, increasing the island's population to just over eight million.[1] Chiang filled all government positions in the National Assembly, the Legislative Yuan and the Control Yuan with mainlanders. Politicians elected on the mainland in 1947 and 1948 were not required to be re-elected in Taiwan since the island was seen as only a province of China. Instead, they were to hold their seats 'indefinitely'. From the 1950s onwards, native Taiwanese competed with mainlanders in local elections, but these polls were merely a way of co-opting the local élite and gaining native Taiwanese support; no serious attempt was made to incorporate local interests into the regime. Ethnic divisions were reinforced by linguistic ones: while mainlanders who arrived after 1949 spoke Mandarin, native Taiwanese spoke either Hoklo or Hakka, both of which were forbidden in schools. The KMT's domination of political and government affairs in Taiwan and its discriminatory ethnic policy were legitimised by the party's claim to mainland sovereignty. Taiwan was a 'province', the KMT regime a 'government in exile'.

By the 1970s, social change and economic development had begun to prompt new demands for political liberalisation. Most Taiwanese had become wealthier and better educated, and the middle class had grown. As a result, new political groups emerged to challenge the KMT. Unlike the 'outside-the-party' (*Tangwai*) candidates who competed in elections in the 1950s and 1960s, this new class of opponents tended to comprise Taiwan-born members of the intelligentsia – lawyers, students and university professors.[2] Campaigning and other political activities expanded from isolated, local interests into more organised, nationwide alliances.

Facing diplomatic isolation abroad and increasing political challenges at home, the KMT became more responsive to local demands. The 'Taiwanisation' process begun in the 1960s accel-

steady 'Taiwanisation' and the rise of Lee Teng-hui

erated, as party, judicial and police organisations made concerted efforts to integrate native Taiwanese. By the mid-1980s, over 70% of the KMT's 2.2m members were native Taiwanese.[3] Taiwan-born Lee was nominated by Chiang as vice-president in 1984 in a bid to rally native support for the regime. Lee had been a popular mayor of Taipei between 1978 and 1981, and governor of Taiwan province in 1981–84. The incorporation of disparate native-Taiwanese interests and social groups into the party machine meant that voices calling for more political reform, and questioning the hitherto unchallenged 'one-China' policy, began to be heard from within the KMT élite itself. In another side-effect of 'Taiwanisation', a native Taiwanese identity and nationalism began to develop, which in turn fuelled the debate on cross-Strait relations.

On 28 September 1986, the DPP announced its formation. In November, the party held its first assembly, and released a draft of its charter and political platform. The main points were:

- establishing the ROC as a sovereign, independent state;
- creating a free and democratic political order;
- instituting educational, social and cultural reforms; and
- pursuing peaceful and independent defence and foreign policies.

Although the formation of political parties was illegal under martial law, the KMT took no action and the party was allowed to participate in legislative elections that December, winning more than 20% of the vote. On 15 July 1987, Chiang lifted martial law and legalised the formation of political parties on condition that they respected the constitution and did not declare independence. A new National Security Law was passed, granting freedom of assembly and association. Chiang took these steps for several reasons. International pressure on the KMT to relax its authoritarian rule had grown, especially from the US Congress. On 1 August 1986, the US House of Representatives Foreign Relations Committee passed a resolution urging the KMT to lift its ban on political parties.[4] Chiang was also responding to demands from Taiwan's increasingly powerful and affluent business community to expand economic relations with China. In addition, the challenge posed by the DPP had made it imperative for Chiang and the KMT to liberalise in order to placate dissent.

The DPP was formed by a coalition of *Tangwai* forces, including moderate politicians, pro-Taiwanese independence (*Taidu*) candidates and labour and welfare activists.[5] In the early 1980s, *Tangwai* activists reconsidered their strategy, and began to concentrate their campaign against the KMT's authoritarianism on Taiwan's ethnic cleavages. The DPP's powerful Formosan faction, for example, came to see ethnic self-determination as an effective issue on which to win electoral support. The DPP thus presented itself as a party for the 'Taiwanese' people, as opposed to the KMT, which, the DPP claimed, was concerned primarily with mainlander interests. As the political environment became more liberal towards the end of the 1980s, a comparatively junior DPP faction, New Tide, tried to put independence at the centre of the DPP's platform. Just before National Assembly elections in December 1991, a resolution was pushed through the party convention to write the goal of independence into the DPP charter.[6] By questioning the 'one-China' principle and highlighting the emergence of a separate Taiwanese identity, the DPP was challenging not only the KMT's vision of the ROC, but also its legitimacy as the representative of the Taiwanese people.

The Lee Teng-hui Factor

Lee became the first Taiwan-born president of the ROC following Chiang's death on 13 January 1988. Many of the KMT's mainlander old guard viewed Lee's succession with suspicion, although the perception that his leadership would only be transitional reduced dissent. Lee's accession transformed the KMT's public face. Eager to establish and consolidate his own authority, he scaled back mainlander influence within the KMT and amended the constitution to remove the executive's right to dissolve political parties.[7] On 3 February 1988, the KMT's Central Standing Committee passed a programme to reform the two elected parliamentary chambers, the National Assembly and the Legislative Yuan. A retirement scheme for veteran legislators was introduced, and the number of directly elected National Assembly seats increased to 225 out of a total of 325. The 'Period of Mobilisation against Communist Rebellion' ended in 1991, and Article 100 of the criminal code, which made it illegal to advocate either Taiwanese independence or communism, was abolished. Lee was treading a fine line: on the one hand, he was trying, at least temporarily, to maintain the KMT's traditional mainland ties and adherence to the 'one-China' principle, while on the other bringing the party more into line with its native-Taiwanese membership.

Lee's attempts at greater political reform alienated many in the KMT. Two competing power blocs took shape within the party, with Lee heading the 'mainstream faction', and mainlander Defence

Minister (and later Premier) Hau Pei-tsun leading the 'non-mainstream' one.[8] The power-struggle between these two blocs in 1990–91 revolved around a number of policy issues. These included whether Taiwan should speed up cultural and economic exchanges with China; whether pro-independence exiles should be allowed to return to Taiwan; and constitutional change. Lee resisted many of the non-mainstream faction's recommendations, such as establishing direct sea and air links with the mainland. At the same time, however, he supported its preference for changing from a parliamentary to a presidential system, favouring popular elections, rather than indirect ones through an electoral college.[9]

Lee's manoeuvrings made it difficult for his opponents in either the KMT or the DPP to flourish. He attracted support from native-Taiwanese politicians, and cited favourable public opinion to fend off his critics. Since the DPP viewed the non-mainstream faction as its chief rival, a tacit coalition developed between the party and Lee. In February 1993, their joint efforts culminated in Hau's replacement as premier by Lien Chan, a native Taiwanese, thus completing the process of Taiwanisation within the KMT élite. Disenchanted KMT legislators led by Chao Shao-kang, who favoured reunification with the mainland and advocated appeasing China, formed the New KMT Alliance, which split from the KMT in August 1993 to become the New Party.

Lee helped to prevent a polarisation of Taiwanese politics by reducing the hostility between mainlanders and native Taiwanese. At the same time, the Taiwanisation of the KMT élite undermined one of the most important planks of the DPP's platform – Taiwanese national identity. Even on the issue of Taiwanese independence, the DPP failed to produce practical policy suggestions that qualitatively differed from the KMT's. Lee also undertook other initiatives aimed at undercutting the DPP. One of the most important was the adoption of 'flexible' or 'pragmatic' diplomacy in Taiwan's international relations.

'Pragmatic Diplomacy'

'Pragmatic diplomacy' was intended to promote Taiwan's 'national development and position in the international community'.[10] These initiatives, which enjoyed popular support in Taiwan, aimed first to undercut the DPP, but they were also designed to test Beijing's tolerance levels.[11] The first set of 'pragmatic' policies aimed at raising Taiwan's international profile. By the 1980s, Taiwan had the world's second-largest foreign-currency reserves, and was ranked twenty-fifth in the world in terms of per-capita gross national product (GNP). In exchange for recognition, the government provided international organisations and governments in Africa and Latin America with generous economic assistance. This so-called 'dollar diplomacy' included setting up an International Economic Development Fund, which made large loans to friendly states such as Poland, the Philippines and Paraguay.[12] Taiwan also sought representation in international economic organisations, ostensibly to safeguard its economic interests. To achieve this, the authorities were willing to relax the traditionally inflexible 'one-China' principle, accepting a 'less-than-statehood' position if doing so would lead to participation in international bodies such as the Asia-Pacific Economic Cooperation (APEC) forum and the Asian Development Bank (ADB). In what amounted to a *de facto* recognition of China by Taipei, a high-level delegation travelled to Beijing to attend the ADB's annual meeting in 1989. Taiwan also dropped its insistence that states with diplomatic relations with China had to relinquish them as a precondition for recognising Taipei. Senior members of the Taiwanese government made informal state visits under the label of 'vacations'.

From 1993, Taiwan also began to push its claim for UN membership. The initiative included an offer to the UN of $1bn for a seat in the General Assembly. As put by Lee, the campaign was based on three principles. First, it was part of Taiwan's quest for a workable relationship with China. Second, Taiwan stressed that it did not seek to represent the whole of China; its UN membership would not challenge Beijing's since it was consistent with the 'one-China, two-political entities' model. Third, Taiwan maintained that it needed to protect the rights of its 21m citizens through the UN.[13] In 1994 and 1995, Taiwan's Government Information Office (GIO) placed large advertisements pressing Taipei's case in influential publications such as the *New York Times*, the *Wall Street Journal*, the London *Times* and *Newsweek*.[14] Despite China's arguments that Taiwan was only a renegade Chinese province, not a sovereign state, Lee persisted with his campaign for UN membership. The majority of Taiwanese supported it, thereby increasing the KMT's electoral appeal against the DPP, as well as sustaining the island's international profile in the face of China's attempts to intensify its isolation.[15]

Democratic Politics and Lee's US Visit

The starkest evidence of the way in which changes in Taiwan's domestic politics affected its relations with China and the US came in mid-1995, when Lee tried to obtain a visa to visit the US. This was not the first time that he had sought to enter the country; on his way to Central America and South Africa in May 1994, Lee had asked permission to enter the US to play golf. He was granted only a transit visa through Hawaii, although a senior State Department official met him at the airport, and Lee was invited to leave the aircraft to rest.[16] Congress and the US press used the incident to condemn the administration for 'mistreating' the elderly leader of democratic and affluent Taiwan; at the end of 1994, Congress passed a resolution urging the administration to allow Lee to visit.

The opportunity for another try arose in early 1995, when Lee was invited by his old university, Cornell in New York, to speak at that year's graduation ceremony. By the time Lee applied for his visa, Taipei believed that President Bill Clinton's China policy was flexible enough to grant it.[17] In mid-term elections in November 1994, the Democratic Party lost its majority in both houses of Congress to the Republicans. Under their new House speaker, Newt Gingrich, Republicans exploited the Taiwan issue to attack the White House. Overwhelming Congressional support for Taiwan's case appeared to make possible an attempt to improve the international profile of both Taiwan, and of Lee himself.

A visit to the US would also boost the domestic political standing of Lee and the KMT ahead of legislative elections in December 1995, and Taiwan's first-ever direct elections for president, scheduled for March 1996. Since the mid-1980s, the KMT's share of the national vote had steadily declined. In Legislative Yuan elections in 1986, 1989 and 1992, the party's support fell from 69% to 59% to 53%, while support for DPP candidates climbed from 25% to 29% and finally to 31%.[18] The rise of the DPP was still more impressive in elections at county and city levels. In local polls in 1985, *Tangwai* candidates won 14% of the vote. By 1989, this had increased to 30%, and it rose again to 41% in 1993. Over the same period, the KMT's share fell from 61% to 47% – the first time the party had scored less than 50%.[19] In December 1994, the KMT polled just 26% in elections for the mayor of Taipei, against 44% for the DPP.[20] One explanation for the KMT's decline lay in Taiwan's democratisation process itself. The need for campaign funding led to the 'institutionalisation' of corruption, involving corporate interests, regional clans, politicians and organised crime. KMT politicians were seen by electors as the major culprits; DPP candidates, by contrast, were viewed as 'cleaner'.[21]

Although the KMT had adopted much of the DPP's platform between 1988 and 1994, and had introduced a number of democratic reforms, both the party and Lee himself appeared to face a hard task in securing votes in the 1995–96 elections. Since 'pragmatic diplomacy' enjoyed domestic support, Lee may have regarded the visit to the US as potentially an election-winning move. Although many in the KMT, including Foreign Minister Frederick Chien, opposed Lee's decision as 'provocative', his quest to become Taiwan's first popularly elected president appeared to make the gamble worthwhile.[22] Neither Washington nor Beijing fully appreciated the extent to which Lee's strategy was driven by domestic political concerns; when the time came for each to respond, serious problems arose.

chapter 3

China and Changing Perceptions of Taiwan

Relations between China and the outside world changed significantly after the end of the Cold War. With the collapse of the Soviet Union in 1991, the shared strategic interests between China and the US largely disappeared, and other issues, such as disputes over human rights, trade and arms proliferation, increased in importance. The repression of pro-democracy demonstrations in Tiananmen Square in June 1989 led the West to reassess China and its political system. US President George Bush's administration imposed sanctions, and Sino-American relations reached their lowest point since normalisation in 1979.[1]

This apparently more hostile external environment coincided with domestic difficulties. In the wake of Tiananmen and the break-up of the Soviet Union, the CCP, although remaining relatively intact, faced a crisis of legitimacy. Greater economic liberalisation following Deng's 'Southern Tour' in 1992 led to a transfer of power from the centre to the regions, and the emergence of separatist movements in sensitive border areas, such as Xinjiang, Tibet and Inner Mongolia. In response to fears that the party could lose its grip on Chinese society, especially as economic reforms began under-cutting its ideology, the CCP looked for new ways to appeal to the population. As the ailing Deng's potential successors jockeyed for position, leaders began to portray themselves as patriots, and to use assertive nationalism in the face of 'foreign imperialists' to rally popular support. Nationalism's wide appeal meant that the sovereignty of the 'renegade province' of Taiwan was a non-negotiable issue, and reunification re-emerged as the foremost national objective. Although *de facto* Taiwanese independence had been tolerated for four decades, *de jure* independence was unacceptable.

US Attitudes

In the first half of the 1990s, Beijing became increasingly convinced that the US was intent on containing, rather than engaging, China. Suspicion that the West would like to see the country's dis-integration bolstered the perception that the outside world was fundamentally hostile.[2] Conversely, the combination of China's threatening talk and increasing economic strength – growth-rates exceeded 10% annually between 1992 and 1995 – alarmed many of the country's neighbours, as well as many in the US.[3]

In 1993, Clinton issued an executive order linking China's Most Favored Nation (MFN) trading status with 'significant overall progress' in human rights.[4] Leaders in Beijing interpreted the policy as an aggressive attempt to interfere in China's internal affairs. Other issues, such as the US rejection of China's bid to host the Olympic Games in 2000, were also taken as evidence of US hostility. In 1993, the US claimed that the Chinese vessel *Yinhe* was transporting chemicals to Iran intended for use in weapons, though no chemicals were found when the boat was inspected. In February 1994, US Assistant Secretary of State for Human Rights John Shattuck met prominent dissident Wei Jingsheng in a hotel in Beijing. A furious China reacted with a number of political arrests on the eve of Secretary of State Warren Christopher's unsuccessful visit in March 1994. During this period, there was little high-level contact between the two sides, other than Christopher's infrequent meetings with Chinese Foreign Minister Qian Qichen at international conferences. In February 1995, the Clinton administration unveiled its report on security strategy for the East Asia-Pacific, fuelling Beijing's suspicions. The report reaffirmed that the US would maintain 100,000 troops in the region, and would strengthen existing bilateral alliances. It also declared that, without 'a better understanding of China's plans, capabilities and intentions, other Asian states may feel a need to respond to China's growing military power ... the United States and China's neighbors would welcome greater transparency in China's defense programs, strategies and doctrines'.[5]

The anti-China opinion that surfaced in the US media further strained Sino-US relations.

US policy towards Taiwan also appeared to be changing. Beijing regarded the US agreement in September 1992 to sell 150 F-16 fighter aircraft to Taiwan as a violation of Sino-US communiqués. According to the joint communiqué of August 1982 (see Appendix, page 77):

> *The US Government states that it does not seek to carry out a long term policy of arms sales to Taiwan, and that its arms sales to Taiwan will not exceed, either in qualitative or in quantitative terms, the level of those supplied in recent years since the establishment of diplomatic relations between the United States and China, and that it intends to reduce gradually its arms sales to Taiwan leading over a period of time to a final resolution.*[6]

After 18 months' preparation, the Clinton administration announced its Taiwan Policy Review (TPR) in September 1994.[7] Under the TPR, the US intended to upgrade its 'unofficial' relations with Taiwan, but without compromising the 'one-China' principle. The administration also tried to eradicate anomalies, such as the fact that US citizens of Taiwanese origin had to give China, not Taiwan, as *the US Taiwan Policy Review* their place of birth. The TPR was criticised by both Beijing and Taipei. For Taiwan, it did not go far enough. It explicitly stated, for example, that senior Taiwanese officials – including the four most senior ones, the president and vice-president, and the head and deputy head of the Executive Yuan – would not be allowed to visit the US, but could only transit the country.[8] Other officials could visit Members of Congress, but would not be allowed to enter the State Department or the White House. The TPR also declared that the US would not support Taiwan's applications to join international organisations where statehood was a membership criterion. Beijing, on the other hand, was unhappy with the legalisation of official cabinet-level meetings. China also disliked the renaming of Taiwan's representation in Washington. Originally entitled the Coordination

Table I *Major US Arms Transfers to Taiwan, 1989–1999*

Order date	Delivery date	Units	Designation
1989	1993–98	7	*Perry* frigate
1990	1993–97	7	CH-47 helicopter
1992	1993–97	63	AH-1W helicopter
1992	1997–	150	F-16A/B ground-attack fighter
1993	1997–98	6	*Patriot* surface-to-air missile
1993	1995–	12	C-130 transport
1994	1998	4	S-70C search-and-rescue helicopter
1994	1997	2	*Newport* tank-landing ship (leased)
1995	1997	32	S-2T reconnaissance vehicle
1995	1996–	300	Ex-US M-60A3 main battle tanks
1995	1998	28	M-109A5 artillery
1996	1998	74	*Avenger* surface-to-air missile
1996	1998	30	TH-67 helicopter
1996	1998	1,299	*Stinger* surface-to-air missile
1997	2000	21	AH-1W helicopter
1997	1997–99	5	*Knox* frigate
1998	2001	13	OH-58D helicopter
1998		58	*Harpoon* anti-surface ship missile
1999	2002	9	CH-47SD helicopter
1999	2002	4	E-2T airborne early-warning aircraft
1999	2003	4	*Aegis* TMD-capable destroyer

Source   IISS

Council of North American Affairs, which gave no indication of connections with Taiwan, the name was changed in October 1994 to the Taipei Economic and Cultural Representative Office (TECRO), which Beijing regarded as upgrading Taiwan's status in the US. Former US Ambassador to China Winston Lord, who was known for his critical views of the CCP regime, was responsible for drafting the TPR, only adding to Beijing's mistrust.

Despite perceptions of a tilt towards Taiwan in US policy, Washington maintained a deliberately ambiguous position concerning the extent of the US military commitment to Taiwan, and the circumstances under which it would be brought into play. Washington opposed unification by force, since this would undermine the US strategic position in East Asia and damage the country's regional credibility. At the same time, the US was reluctant to offer Taiwan the opportunity to declare independence beneath a US security umbrella. It also recognised the broader strategic need to maintain a working relationship with China. Powerful business lobbies in the US worked hard to ensure that functional Sino-US relations would be maintained. This deliberate ambiguity became more difficult to sustain following the November 1994 elections. The new, majority-Republican Congress was bent on challenging Clinton on many issues, including his China policy. Politics in the US, as well as in Taiwan, were once again a major factor in relations with China.

Asian Attitudes

Although Japan was one of the first states to lift sanctions against China after the Tiananmen massacre, Sino-Japanese relations deteriorated badly in the early 1990s. As with the US, Japan's official 'one-China' policy came under strain as Taiwan's international diplomatic and economic activities increased. Deepening economic relations between Japan and Taiwan, and the two countries' membership of APEC, gave rise to new and difficult diplomatic situations. One such was an official meeting between Taiwan's Economic Minister, Chiang Ping-kun, and Japanese International Trade Minister Ryutaro Hashimoto in October 1994. Taiwanese Foreign Minister Chien had paid a 'private' visit to Japan in 1993, but Chiang's visit was the first by a Taiwanese in an official capacity since 1972. In September 1994, Japan's Ministry of Foreign Affairs allowed a visit from Taiwanese Vice-Premier Hsu Li-teh in connection with the Asian Games in Hiroshima. In response, China threatened to thwart Japan's bid for permanent membership of the UN Security Council – a threat which Japanese officials chose to ignore. The government had made an earlier concession to Beijing by not inviting Lee to attend the games, despite a petition to that effect from 110 members of the Diet. Tensions between China and Japan over Taiwan increased against the background of a general deterioration in Sino-Japanese relations. While both parties recognised the importance of their economic links, other issues, such as Chinese nuclear tests, Beijing's perceived military build-up and territorial disputes, all caused problems. In response to China's tests, Japan cut grant aid from ¥7.8bn to ¥500m in 1995.[9]

China's relations with its South-east Asian neighbours were also becoming more complicated, notably over territorial issues in the South China Sea. Beijing was reluctant to resolve disputes through a multilateral security dialogue, as favoured by the Association of South-East Asian Nations (ASEAN), preferring instead unilateral action and bilateral talks. Ostensibly, China refused to become involved in multilateral fora because Taiwan was also a South China Sea claimant, and hence an unacceptable participant. Political difficulties aside, many South-east Asian states welcomed Taiwan's attempts to diversify its foreign investment away from China. Taipei's acceptance of dual recognition allowed informal visits to ASEAN states by senior Taiwanese officials. In January 1994, Premier Lien visited Malaysia, where he met Prime Minister Mahathir Mohamad, and Singapore, meeting Senior Minister Lee Kuan Yew. Also in 1994, Lee Teng-hui visited the Philippines, Indonesia and Thailand.[10]

Beijing's Perspective

Although China initially mistrusted Lee's native-Taiwanese background, he was nonetheless regarded as 'someone Beijing could do business with'.[11] However, as his policies unfolded, Beijing gradually became more suspicious of his intentions, and began to reassess his past. His educational background was questioned because it paralleled that of Peng Ming-min, one of the most prominent leaders of Taiwan's independence movement. Peng, who was arrested in 1964, had remained in contact with Lee during his ensuing exile in the US. In April 1990, when Lee was attempting to consolidate power in his own right, he allegedly sent a 'sincerely worded' message to Peng urging him to return to Taiwan.[12] Lee's ousting of pro-unification elements in the KMT was reinterpreted in Beijing as an effort to persuade Peng to come home. Lien, a native Taiwanese and one-time student of Peng, had visited his former teacher in the US; when Peng finally returned to Taiwan in late 1992, Lien twice attended welcoming parties and drank a toast to him.[13] For Beijing, this appeared to support suspicions that Lee was secretly encouraging organisations advocating Taiwanese independence.[14]

A key point in Beijing's changing assessment of Lee came in April 1994, when he was interviewed by Japanese journalist and personal friend Ryotaro Shiba.[15] In the interview, published in the Japanese magazine *Asahi Weekly*, Lee spoke of his affinity with Japanese, as opposed to Chinese, culture. He referred to Moses and the Book of

Lee redefines 'one-China'

Exodus in connection with the people of Taiwan, and described the KMT as an *émigré* regime. Lee further expounded on Taiwan's new position later in 1994, when he called on China to accept that Taiwan was a separate political entity, with jurisdiction over a different part of China. 'One-China', he argued, should no longer be regarded as a meaningful political entity, but as a historical, geographical, cultural and racial one.[16] In response, Jiang issued an eight-point proposal on cross-Strait relations on 30 January 1995. The proposal stated that Beijing would:

- adhere to the principle of 'one-China' as the basis for peaceful reunification;
- allow non-governmental economic and cultural ties between Taiwan and other countries, while opposing Taiwan's efforts to 'expand its living space internationally';
- talk with the Taiwanese authorities about any matter, on the premise that there is only 'one-China';
- not renounce the use of force, although this would be directed against the 'schemes of foreign forces to interfere with China's reunification', rather than against Taiwan;
- make efforts to expand economic exchanges and cooperation with Taiwan; and

- fully respect the lifestyle, rights and interests of the 'compatriots in Taiwan', and their wish to be 'masters of their country'.

Jiang also declared that Taiwan's leaders were welcome to visit the mainland in 'appropriate capacities', and that the 'splendid culture of five thousand years ... constitutes an important basis for the peaceful reunification of the motherland'.[17] In his reply, issued in April, Lee stressed that negotiations to end hostilities across the Strait could not take place unless China renounced force. He again emphasised Taiwan's sovereignty, and suggested that both sides should be allowed to participate in international organisations. Lee did, however, appear more cooperative on other issues, such as agreeing to meet the CCP leadership in Beijing and considering establishing direct air and sea links with the mainland. China bluntly denounced Lee's response and, in April 1995, declined Taiwan's offer to host a meeting of 'negotiating groups' to discuss cross-Strait issues.

As Taiwanese democratisation gathered pace in the 1990s, China's position became increasingly difficult. Taiwanese policy was becoming more unpredictable, while the government's democratic mandate directly challenged Chinese political practices and the CCP's legitimacy. Ethnic groups in China drew inspiration from the DPP's policy of ethnic-Taiwanese self-determination and Lee's erosion of mainlander influence in the KMT. Finally, a democratic and prosperous Taiwan was attracting greater international sympathy. The stage was thus set for a robust Chinese response to its weakening position.

chapter 4

The 1995–96 Taiwan Crisis

In retrospect, crises rarely appear as neat or as obvious as they do when they are unfolding. But the crisis in the Taiwan Strait in 1995–96 was a messy affair even as it took place, and with hindsight appears all the more risky and uncertain. The main cause of these problems was the fact that much of the crisis was driven by the domestic politics of all three actors involved, particularly developments in Taiwan.

US Domestic Politics

On 22 May 1995, the US announced that Lee had been granted a visa to enter the country as a private individual on 8–12 June. The previous March, the State Department had declared that no such visa would be issued, prompting mounting criticism in Congress and the media; both drew comparisons between Lee's case and the decision to admit Sinn Fein leader Gerry Adams on 9 March. Despite this pressure, the State Department continued to assure Chinese representatives in the US, and the Chinese Ministry of Foreign Affairs (MFA), that Lee would not be granted a visa.[1] At a UN meeting on 16 April 1995, Secretary of State Christopher insisted to Chinese Foreign Minister Qian that US policy had not changed. He also indicated that Congressional pressure regarding Taiwan was a 'very serious problem', perhaps hoping to warn Beijing that the State Department's view might not prevail.

This was indeed the case. On 2 May, the House of Representatives voted unanimously in favour of granting Lee an entry visa; the Senate followed six days later, voting 91 to one. Members of Congress then threatened to pass a binding resolution inviting Lee for an official – rather than private – visit, a move which could have been even more disastrous for Sino-US relations. Christopher, Secretary of Defense William Perry and National Security Council Advisor Anthony Lake, all of whom had originally recommended refusing Lee a visa, agreed that it should now be granted.

Following the announcement that a visa was to be issued, State Department and other officials repeatedly tried to assure Beijing that fundamental US policy had not changed, that the mainstay of Clinton's China policy remained 'constructive engagement', and that the mechanisms of democratic politics had left the White House with limited options. Despite these efforts, Beijing's response was hostile, and Christopher's credibility with Qian collapsed.[2] The sudden announcement embarrassed the MFA, which had a more sophisticated understanding than other parts of the government of the US policy process.[3] The ministry issued a strong protest on 23 May, which accused the US of 'causing' the creation of 'two Chinas', violating the 'one-China' principle of the three joint communiqués and jeopardising Sino-US relations.[4] The visa decision was regarded as confirmation that US policy had shifted from engagement to containment, and that the US was seeking to heighten Taiwan's international profile. A delegation led by People's Liberation Army (PLA) air force commander Yu Zhengwu abruptly ended its visit to the US, and returned to China. On 26 May, Beijing 'postponed' the scheduled visit of Chinese Defence Minister Chi Haotian to the US and, two days later, announced the suspension of talks, specifically negotiations on arms control and proliferation, and on nuclear-energy cooperation.[5]

Washington nonetheless continued to hope that, once the rhetoric subsided, normal relations would resume. This view appeared to be supported when Tang Shubei, the vice-chairman of ARATS, went ahead with his scheduled trip to Taiwan, arriving in Taipei just four days after the visa decision.[6] However, this merely reflected the fact that China's anger was directed more at Washington than at Taipei. Tang's unchanged schedule may also have indicated the extent to which Beijing's decision-making process was shocked into immobility by the visa decision.

Although Lee's visit was to be the first to the US by a sitting president of the ROC, Washington nonetheless hoped that it would remain low-profile in order to limit the diplomatic damage.[7] Taiwanese officials, including Benjamin Lu, Taipei's representative in Washington, gave assurances to the State

Lee's talk of 'popular sovereignty' at Cornell

Department that Lee's trip would indeed be non-political. However, during his speech at Cornell's graduation ceremony, Lee used the phrase 'The Republic of China on Taiwan', a formulation regarded as provocative by both Beijing and Washington, 17 times. Lee's talk of 'popular sovereignty' was also seen in Beijing as part of his apparent pursuit of Taiwanese independence. China was disturbed by the high profile of Lee's visit: over the six days of his trip, global news coverage totalled 949 articles, 239 of them in the North American press.[8] Beijing's mood was not improved when, just three days after Lee's return on 12 June, Premier Lien began a visit to Austria, Hungary and the Czech Republic. On 16 June, Li Daoyu, the Chinese ambassador to the US, was recalled to 'report on his work' – a strong reaction not anticipated in Washington.[9] On the same day, ARATS notified the SEF that the Koo–Wang talks scheduled for late July would be cancelled, effectively breaking off relations with Taiwan. The US began to relay messages between the two sides. On 12 July, Lake met Liu Huaqiu, the director of China's State Council Office of Foreign Affairs and, four days later, met Ding Mou-shih, the head of Taiwan's National Security Council. Meetings such as these were held throughout the ensuing crisis.

From mid-1995, there were indications that Lee, prompted by Washington, toned down Taiwan's military posture.[10] Lee's concerns were not, however, shared in Beijing. On 18 July, China's official news agency Xinhua announced that, from 21 July, the PLA would conduct five days of missile tests. These would take place 150km off Taiwan's northern coast, demonstrating Beijing's policy of 'military force for the protection of Taiwan'.[11] More live-fire exercises were held between 15 and 25 August, during which six missiles were fired into the test area. After these exercises, the US administration issued no public warnings over China's actions in a bid to avoid strengthening hardliners in Beijing. From the outset, Washington was confident that China would not have the will, intent or capability to initiate direct military action against Taiwan or its surrounding islands.[12] At the same time, the administration may have felt that Taiwan needed reminding that its 'pragmatic diplomacy' could have serious consequences.[13]

Throughout the latter half of 1995, Beijing sought assurances that Washington would not again grant Lee, or other top Taiwanese leaders, permission to enter the US.[14] It also urged Washington to issue another joint communiqué. The US refused to comply. On 1 August, Christopher met Qian at an ASEAN summit in Brunei, and delivered a letter from Clinton to Jiang. Christopher made no concrete promises, but reaffirmed past US policy on Taiwan, and stated that 'the United States has not and does not intend to change its long-standing one-China policy'.[15] Following the Qian–Christopher meeting, there were signs of improvement in Sino-US relations. Beijing indicated its approval of the appointment of James Sasser, the US ambassador-designate to China.[16] Human-rights activist Harry Wu was released in August following Washington's agreement that Hillary Clinton would take part in the International Women's Conference in Beijing in September. Li, the Chinese ambassador to the US, returned to Washington in October. This improvement in relations reflected a shift in Beijing's perceptions of the source of Taiwan's apparent independence agenda. Instead of blaming 'international forces' for playing the 'Taiwan card' to isolate and contain China, leaders in Beijing began to see that the real challenge came from the new Taiwanese leaders, such as Lee and the *Taidu* activists.

At a meeting in Beidaihe in late August 1995, civilian and military leaders agreed to a further round of exercises near Taiwan in the run-up to legislative elections on the island in December.[17] By this time, criticism of Jiang's eight-point proposal, which hardliners regarded as too conciliatory, had become louder. But Beijing also continued to seek assurances from the US that no further visas would be issued. Both sides portrayed a meeting between Clinton and Jiang on 24 October in New York as largely positive, despite early disagreements over protocol and location.[18] Jiang restated Chinese sensitivities over Taiwan, while Clinton 'reaffirmed in general terms the pursuit of a one-China policy'. As with Christopher in August, Clinton did not give specific or concrete guarantees that no further visits by senior Taiwanese officials would take place, only that they would be 'considered on a case-by-case basis', and would be unofficial, private and rare.[19] On 14–18 November, Joseph Nye, Assistant Secretary of Defense for International Security Affairs, travelled to Beijing for talks; China agreed to host a previously rebuffed visit by Under-Secretary of State Peter Tarnoff, and to proceed with a postponed Sino-US summit. Taiwan dominated the agenda during Nye's trip. PLA leaders strongly hinted at a revision of military plans concerning Taiwan. Despite Chinese probing, Nye and his group refused to discuss 'contingency planning', stating only that any military action against Taiwan would be a serious mistake.[20] Nye also reiterated the US commitment to the Taiwan Relations Act.

Nye's warnings came too late. On 15 November, the PLA began the largest and most complex amphibious manoeuvres ever undertaken in the Taiwan Strait. The exercises were planned directly by the Central Military Commission (CMC), with operational planning involving staff officers from all of China's military regions. They continued for ten days, and included a simulated invasion of Dongshan Island off the coast of southern Fujian. Between 16,000 and 18,000 military personnel participated, and 200 landing craft and 100 other vessels were mobilised. On 1 December, the day before the Taiwanese went to the polls, Beijing warned of further exercises, including large-scale simulated attacks and bombing runs.

Although Taiwan's legislative elections took place under the cloud of Chinese military threats and exercises, it is difficult to demonstrate that Beijing's actions influenced the outcome. In accordance with pre-election opinion surveys, the KMT suffered its most serious setback, losing seven seats to bring its total in the Legislative Yuan to 85 out of 164. The pro-unification New Party tripled its seats, from seven held by KMT defectors to 21, while the DPP gained four seats, bringing its total to 54.

Actions and Reactions

For all the parties concerned, the legislative elections were merely the run-up to the main contest. On 19 December 1995, the US aircraft carrier *Nimitz, en route* from Japan to the Persian Gulf, sailed through the Taiwan Strait, the first US carrier to do so for 17 years. Officially, the US maintained that the course was the result of an operational decision based on weather conditions. It is likely, however, that the political context was taken into account; certainly, the commander of the Pacific Fleet, Admiral Ronald J. Zlatoper, sought guidance from the White House, which endorsed the decision.[21] Neither the PLA nor the Taiwanese military appeared to detect the passage of the *Nimitz*, although the PLA did note other US ships travelling through the Strait, leading to a private protest

the significance of the Nimitz episode

from Beijing. In January 1996, US intelligence leaked the news of the *Nimitz*'s passage to its Taiwanese counterpart, which promptly passed it on to the press.[22] A public announcement six weeks later was authorised by Pacific Fleet headquarters in Hawaii.[23]

The *Nimitz* episode was an important signal to Beijing that the US continued to regard the Taiwan Strait as international waters. A speech by Nye to the Asia Society in Seattle on 12 December 1995 was, however, less clear-cut. Nye stressed that 'nobody knows' how the US would respond to a Taiwan Strait conflict, though both sides should be aware of the 'grave danger' and the serious risk of escalation. Nye's statements could be interpreted as suggesting the possibility of, but not a commitment to, US intervention in the event of conflict.[24] China was in no mood to heed vague warnings. At the end of October 1995, former Assistant Secretary of Defense Chas W. Freeman was told by senior Chinese generals that China was planning one practice missile firing a day for 30 days. The exercises would begin the week following presidential elections in Taiwan on 23 March 1996. Freeman also reported 'theoretical' discussions with Chinese officials about the possible use of nuclear weapons against the US, should it intervene. Freeman reported to Lake on 4 January 1996.[25] Eight days later, Lake and Liu met and, on 16 January, Lake met Ding in New York.

According to the US Office of Naval Intelligence, the PLA began deployment for the forthcoming exercises on 4 February.[26] Troops and aircraft from all over China poured into the Nanjing 'War Zone'. Under the new Nanjing command, elements from all three of the PLA navy's fleets were activated, and air-defence units armed with SA-10B missiles were transferred to the exercise area. On 7 February, an alarmed Tarnoff warned Chinese Vice-Foreign Minister Li Zhaoxing, in Washington at the time, against aggression towards Taiwan, and cited US commitments under the TRA.[27] Li's alleged response reiterated a familiar Beijing stance: 'Taiwan is part of China, and the Taiwan issue is China's internal affair, and no foreign force and no foreign country should interfere'.[28] Briefing Congress on 7 February, both Lord and Kurt Campbell, Deputy Assistant Secretary of Defense for Asian and Pacific Affairs, repeated the US commitment to the TRA, and suggested that Washington was closely monitoring events. Lord stated that the US remained confident that the military exercises did not reflect the 'intention to take military action against Taiwan … the Taiwan authorities have reached the same judgement'.[29]

By the beginning of March, 150,000 PLA troops were gathered for the coming exercises, and 300 aircraft had moved to within striking distance of Taiwan.[30] The Xinhua news agency announced that the first wave of missile exercises would be held on 8–15 March – just after the start of the three-week campaign period before Taiwan's 23 March elections. These firings would take place more than 80km closer to Taiwan than the 1995 exercises; both Clinton and the US Congress publicly condemned the proximity to the island of the two impact areas.[31]

On 7 March, US reconnaissance aircraft and the cruiser *Bunker Hill* monitored technical data transmissions from three Chinese M-9 ballistic missiles to ground-stations tracking their flight.[32] The M-9s, which belonged to the Second Artillery, the nuclear rocket force, landed in shipping lanes adjacent to Taiwan's commercial ports: first Kaohsiung in the south, then Chilung in the north, and then south again to Kaohsiung.[33] Hong Kong's *Wen Wei Po* newspaper, widely regarded as a mouthpiece for Beijing during the crisis, suggested that the PLA sought to serve two purposes with its war games. First, they were designed to improve the PLA's capabilities; and second, they were an attempt to demonstrate China's military strength and its ability to contain Taiwan.[34] By choosing to target areas adjacent to Taiwan's northern and southern ports, China was indicating that it could blockade key maritime and air access routes.

At a State Department banquet in Washington on the evening of 7 March, Perry warned Liu of 'grave consequences' if Chinese weapons hit Taiwan, and told him 'very clearly and very unequiv-ocally' of the US belief that the missile firings were 'reckless'.[35] Perry also informed Liu that China was clearly 'bracketing' Taiwan, a targeting technique that could precede a direct attack.[36] According to

US officials, Liu seemed genuinely surprised by such a strong reaction. The following day, Perry announced that a battle group led by the aircraft carrier *Independence* had been deployed to within 'a few hundred miles' of Taiwan.[37] Undeterred, Xinhua announced on 9 March that a second wave of PLA exercises would take place. These were to be live-fire exercises by air, land and naval forces between 12 and 22 March. They would be held over a large diamond-shaped area off the coast of southern Fujian, close to the psychologically important mid-line of the Taiwan Strait. On 10 March, Christopher issued another serious warning, speaking of 'grave consequences'. While Sino-US tension increased, secret diplomacy between Beijing and Taipei sought to avoid the possibility of any misunderstanding. Bangkok's *Asia Times* reported that, on 10 March, Liu met Lee Teng-hui confidant Lee Yuan-tseh, the president of the government-funded research institute Academia Sinica, for talks in Washington.[38]

diplomatic and military crisis

On 11 March, the Pentagon announced that a second aircraft-carrier battle group, headed by the *Nimitz*, had joined the *Independence* off Taiwan. Although Chinese officials attempted to downplay the nature of the exercises during meetings with State Department and Department of Defense officials, Washington remained unsure as to how far Beijing's provocation would go.[39] If China had either misread or ignored previous signals, sending a second carrier should, according to Deputy Assistant Secretary of Defense Michael Doubleday, 'make sure that there [was] no miscalculation on the part of the Chinese as to our interest in the area'. It would also reassure friends of the US in the region that Washington would 'maintain an interest in ... peace and stability' there.[40] On 12 March, the MFA condemned the deployment of the two carriers. Three days later, Xinhua announced a third wave of exercises from 18 until 25 March, two days after Taiwan's presidential elections. On 17 March, Premier Li Peng warned that the US show of force in the Taiwan Strait was futile, and would only complicate the situation.[41] In the event, bad weather forced the cancellation of most of these manoeuvres. China's war games in the Taiwan Strait ended on 25 March.

As with the legislative elections in 1995, Beijing's actions appeared to have little effect on Taiwanese voters. Lee won the

March polls with 54%. Peng, the DPP's pro-independence challenger, secured 21%, while pro-Beijing New Party candidate Ling Tang-Kang polled only 15%. Many DPP voters appeared to have switched their allegiance to Lee, deeming him the best candidate to deal with the mainland. In concurrent elections for the expanded National Assembly's 334 seats, the KMT won 183, with 49.7% of the vote, the DPP 99 with 29.9%, and the New Party 46, with 13.7%. Lee's victory, and the poor showing of the New Party, were serious blows for Beijing, which had been portraying the president as a dangerous leader taking Taiwan towards independence. Although China did not actually use force, it emerged from the crisis with its reputation for using crude diplomacy and making unreasonable demands enhanced.

chapter 5

No Change, No Solution

In one sense, the crisis of 1995–96 came to a swift conclusion: the Taiwanese held their elections, and the Chinese and Americans stood down their military forces. But in a more important sense, the episode was merely one dangerous moment in a long-term struggle. In the years following, the core of the strategic problem has remained unchanged. Taiwan's domestic political development is gradually pulling the island away from reunification with China. Leaders in Beijing remain uncertain as to how to respond, but know that their nationalist agenda gives them little scope for compromise. The US is wary of becoming more deeply involved than it must in cross-Strait relations. Washington wishes to see neither the use of force by Beijing, nor a rapid move by Taiwan towards formal independence. While the US recognises that its policy of 'strategic ambiguity' towards Taiwan complicates its efforts to deter China, it also knows that a degree of ambiguity must remain, with all the attendant problems for crisis management. It is thus not surprising that little has changed.

After the Crisis

Diplomacy swiftly resumed after China's exercises in the Strait ended. In his inaugural speech on 20 May, Lee made it clear that Taiwanese independence was 'unnecessary' and 'impossible'. He also offered to visit the mainland to 'meet and directly exchange opinions with the Chinese Communist leaders to open new dialogue and co-operation'.[1] But he remained defiant about reunification in the foreseeable future. Despite the smooth handover of Hong Kong from the UK to China on 1 July 1997, Lee dismissed Beijing's 'one-country, two-systems' concept as 'wishful thinking', and vowed 'never to abandon [Taiwan's] democratic institutions'.[2] In an interview with the *Washington Post* after Jiang's high-profile visit to the US in October–November 1997, Lee described Taiwan as 'an independent and sovereign country'.[3]

In keeping with past pragmatic compromises in relations between China and Taiwan, tourism, trade and other exchanges continued to increase despite difficult political relations. The day after Lee's election victory on 23 March, Taiwanese Economic Minister Chiang announced that a proposal would be submitted to the Legislative Yuan in June to ease Taiwan's 47-year ban on direct trade with China. In 1997, trade across the Strait enjoyed double-digit growth, reaching $26bn.[4] The following year, the value of trade stood at $24bn, and at $14bn for the first seven months of 1999. Between January and June 1999, 930,000 Taiwanese visited the mainland, and 54,000 mainlanders travelled to Taiwan.[5] Direct shipping links between Kaohsiung in Taiwan and the Chinese port of Xiamen were established in April 1996. Lee Ching-ping, a deputy director of the SEF, led a private delegation to the mainland in May 1997, where he held talks with ARATS vice-chairman Tang. Representatives from Taiwan's three main political parties attended a conference hosted by the Chinese Academy of Social Sciences in Yantai, Shandong province, in June 1997, where they held extensive discussions with China's Taiwan experts, often in venues outside the meeting.[6]

Taiwan's Politics Changes Shape

As the sense of crisis faded, political forces in Taiwan reflected on what had changed. Most striking was the extent to which the island's parties groped for a new level of consensus regarding cross-Strait relations and domestic politics. Although Taiwan's economy was only briefly affected by the crisis, all political forces nonetheless recognised the island's vulnerability to Chinese actions. Taiwan reportedly suffered capital flight of $12.4bn in the second half of 1995, a record for a six-month period.[7]

The pro-independence DPP began to rethink its policy towards China after the March 1996 elections. Following his poor showing in the polls, Peng left the DPP to form the splinter Taiwan Independence Party. The defeated Formosan-faction candidate in the DPP presidential primaries, Hsu Hsin-Liang, stayed with the party, becoming its chairman in July 1996. In order to increase the DPP's electability, Hsu began to steer the party towards 'representing the mainstream values of the society', promising to adopt policies 'in Taiwan's best interest', and to 'protect [its] security'.[8] Under the leadership of the Formosan faction, the DPP accepted inclusion in the cross-party National Development Conference (NDC), which was convened in December 1996. The DPP put forward a number of principles at the NDC designed to build cross-party consensus on relations with China. These included making the welfare and security of Taiwanese citizens a priority; continuing trade and development with China to meet Taiwanese business needs, including opening the three 'direct links' (post, trade and transport); and preparations for a new phase of talks. Negotiations under the 'one-China' principle were unacceptable to the DPP, but official talks could be held.

Hsu maintained the DPP's moderate position on cross-Strait relations in the run-up to local elections on 29 November 1997. The party also campaigned on more immediate domestic issues, such as law and order, the economy, corruption and criminal involvement in politics. The DPP won 43% of the vote, against 42% for the KMT, giving it 12 of the 23 posts contested. The party immediately repositioned itself as an advocate for cross-Strait peace and stability. In Washington on 9 December 1997, Hsu pledged that if the DPP became the ruling party, it would not seek a plebiscite to determine whether the people of Taiwan wished to secede from China. Instead, he suggested that the DPP's pro-independence stance was interesting only as 'an historical relic'; in power, the party would maintain the status quo.[9] Taiwan's independence, a centre-piece of the DPP's platform since its inception, would be shelved. Hsu conceded that cordial relations across the Strait were essential to Taiwan's economic health and social stability. He also argued that the DPP would try to promote economic ties with Beijing, particularly the three 'direct links'.[10] Thus, the DPP's emphasis switched from advocating independence to acknowledging that Taiwan was a *de facto* independent and sovereign country.

Hsu's modifications of DPP policy soon became more formal reforms. In a DPP seminar on mainland policy on 13–15 February 1998, a new formula – 'strong base and westward advance' – emerged. This was a compromise between the Formosan faction, which advocated improving economic ties, civilian and technical exchanges and progress towards official negotiations ('westward advance'), and the New Tide faction, which called for first developing a strong domestic economy and sense of national identity and civic consciousness ('strong base'). Ironically, the New Tide's position was close to the KMT's mainland policy. More importantly, the compromise cemented a consensus within the DPP that negotiations with Beijing on all issues were necessary. The DPP attacked the distinction drawn by the KMT between 'political' and 'practical' matters, although the party agreed that discussions on sensitive issues like sovereignty should be postponed.

the DPP becomes more pragmatic

Although Hsu was replaced in June 1998 by veteran secessionist and New Tide leader Lin Yih-shyong, in practice the DPP maintained his more moderate policies. The party was slowly dragging itself into the centre-ground of Taiwanese politics – the only place from which it could win presidential elections, scheduled for March 2000. It faced a daunting task: according to an opinion poll conducted by the DPP in October 1998, the party was still regarded as Taiwan's most polemical. Only 6% trusted it to ensure national security, compared with 52% for the KMT. Over 40% felt that the KMT was best-equipped to tackle Taiwan's political isolation, against 9% who favoured the DPP. More than twice as many respondents believed that the KMT was best able to guide Taiwan's political development. On a more positive note for the DPP, Taiwanese electors tend to be influenced more by personality than by party. In addition, the same poll showed that domestic issues such as crime, social order and the environment were the overriding priority of the majority of respondents. Only 12% saw national security as among the top two election issues.[11]

As the 2000 polls approached, Taiwan's politicians became increasingly preoccupied with domestic issues. The elections for the mayor of Taipei, which, together with Legislative Yuan and city-council polls, took place on 5 December 1998, were regarded as an early dress rehearsal for the presidential race. The popular incumbent, Chen Shui-bian of the DPP, was widely tipped to keep the post. He was also favourite to win the DPP's candidacy for president. Chen kept his distance from the DPP's 'strong base and westward advance' position. Instead, he adopted a flexible approach to the independence issue, hoping that ambiguity would increase his appeal. Chen was nonetheless narrowly defeated by his KMT opponent, former Justice Minister and Harvard law graduate Ma Ying-jeou, who won 51.13% of the vote against Chen's 46%. Hong Kong-born Ma's campaign attempted to create a more ethnically inclusive atmosphere, whereas the DPP had emphasised the differences between mainlanders and native Taiwanese. In the legislative elections, the KMT maintained its majority, taking 123 of the 225 seats with 55% of the vote, a 4% increase. The DPP won 70 seats, with its share of the vote rising slightly, from 28% to 31%.[12] Support for the pro-unification New Party collapsed, from 10% to 5%, and it won only 11 seats. Smaller parties and independents took the remaining 21. In the mayoral vote in Taiwan's second city Kaohsiung, DPP candidate Frank Hsieh narrowly defeated KMT incumbent Wu Den-yih.

The elections strengthened the KMT, reversing the decline that had culminated in its defeat in local elections in 1997. The polls also showed popular support for the party's policy towards China, and for its economic management during the financial crisis which began in July 1997. The KMT was firmly re-established as the party of the middle ground. By contrast, the elections demonstrated that the DPP had failed to find any new policies with which to distinguish itself from the KMT.

Jiang Consolidates Power

The contrast between the domestic political and social order in Taiwan and that in China was a major reason why the two parties remained so far apart, and unlikely to find a compromise to ease tensions. The most important feature of mainland politics in the aftermath of the 1995–96 crisis was Jiang's consolidation of power; he ousted Qiao Shi, his main competitor, from the Standing Committee of the Political Bureau at the CCP's Fifteenth Party

Congress in September 1997. In addition, unlike his predecessors, he nominated no military figures to sit on the Standing Committee, possibly signifying a separation between the role of the military and that of civilian leaders. Jiang's visit to the US in October–November 1997 further raised his prestige, especially at home, while the nomination of an economic technocrat, Zhu Rongji, as premier at the Ninth National People's Congress in March 1998 demonstrated the regime's continued commitment to reform.

From early 1998, China stepped up its public calls for Taiwan to restart negotiations, which had been suspended since Beijing cancelled the Koo–Wang talks in June 1995. Taiwan had been reluctant to resume negotiations, primarily because of Beijing's insistence that Taipei accept the 'one-China' principle first, thereby according the island an inferior status. Since this was unacceptable to Taipei, Beijing put forward a looser interpretation of what 'one-China' actually meant, suggesting that the phrase could refer only to geography, rather than to the PRC as a political entity. However, in response to Jiang's call at the Fifteenth Party Congress for an end to hostilities, and for negotiations in accordance with the 'one-China' principle, Lee suggested that 'the Republic of China must first be recognised as a sovereign state', and that 'it seems that the two sides of the strait have no political issues to talk about'.[13]

Following Jiang's visit to the US in late 1997, Washington's 'encouragement' of Taiwan to resume talks increased. In January 1998, former US officials, among them former Defense Secretary Perry, former chairman of the Joint Chiefs of Staff John Shalikashvili, former National Security Advisor Brent Scowcroft and former Commander-in-Chief of US Pacific Forces Ronald Hayes, paid a 'private' visit to Taiwan, following stop-overs in China. The group reportedly carried with them two messages: first, the US would not defend Taiwan against an attack by China if Taipei declared independence; and second, Taiwan should restart negotiations with Beijing. This contravened a US assurance, given in 1982, which stated that Taipei would not be pushed into negotiations with Beijing.[14] The group also allegedly delivered a message from Wang, suggesting that Beijing might consider a still-looser conception of 'one-China' as a cultural, rather than geographical or political, concept. Lake also urged Lee to

new US pressure on Taiwan

resume talks when he travelled to Taipei on 4–8 March, citing the Middle East and Northern Ireland as cases where adversaries had successfully discussed smaller differences, before moving on to deal with more sensitive issues.[15]

Beijing and Taipei finally resumed negotiations on 21–22 April 1998, when a delegation from the SEF led by Jan Jyh-horng met ARATS official Li Yafei at a hotel in Beijing. As in the past, the negotiations were important symbolically, but yielded little of substance. Beijing had abandoned its insistence on political talks, accepting that, as long as there was a will to extend discussions to include more sensitive political issues, lower-level talks would suffice in the short term. On 24 July, Li led a delegation comprising three ARATS officials and a group of Beijing teachers to Taipei, where he urged the SEF formally to respond to ARATS' proposal to broaden the scope of exchanges. He also suggested that political negotiations should begin.[16] SEF chairman Koo led a 12-strong SEF group to China on 14–19 October, meeting Wang in Shanghai. On 18 October, Koo held meetings in Beijing with Vice-Premier and former Foreign Minister Qian, and with Jiang in his capacity as CCP General Secretary. These talks were the highest-level discussions between the two sides since the KMT retreated to Taiwan in 1949.

The negotiations were an important public-relations exercise for Taipei. Its switch from 'no political discussion' to a generally flexible approach demonstrated to the international community that Taiwan was not the trouble-maker in relations across the Strait. But the talks did little more than restore contacts: there was no official breakthrough, no joint declaration and no communiqué was signed. As Taiwanese Premier Vincent Siew pointed out during a meeting of the cabinet and the MAC on 2 November, relations between the rivals remained unaffected.[17] Meanwhile, Siew dismissed Beijing's attempts to woo Taiwan's handful of diplomatic allies as 'two-faced tactics', as Tonga switched its ties to Beijing, following South Africa, the Central African Republic and Guinea-Bissau earlier in the year. At a conference on 2 November, Lee stated that Taiwan's links with China needed as much attention as the island's economic and political development, and that Taipei would keep 'questing for mutual trust and increased friendly ties' with the mainland.[18] Vice-Foreign Minister David Lee announced that Taiwan would continue high-level visits to exchange views with foreign leaders and senior officials, raising Taiwan's international visibility and 'combating China's plot' to 'isolate' Taipei.[19]

US Problems and Policies

If domestic forces in Taiwan and China precluded any new solutions, so too was the US, the leading outside power, unable to achieve a breakthrough. For Washington, the Taiwan problem was part of a wider relationship with China and an increasingly important East Asia. The US priority was to maintain regional stability. In the immediate aftermath of the 1995–96 crisis, this meant focusing on relations with Japan. Even here, however, there were consequences for the management of the Taiwan issue.

Japanese Prime Minister Ryutaro Hashimoto and Clinton reaffirmed the significance of the US–Japan security relationship in April 1996. At the core of this relationship was a new Japan–US Joint Declaration on Security, which proclaimed as its goals ensuring regional security, and building a stable, broad and durable security structure for the Asia-Pacific. The alliance was described as 'bilateral policy co-ordination, including studies on dealing jointly with situations that may emerge in the areas surrounding Japan and which will have important influence on the peace and security of Japan'.[20] On 23 September 1997, Tokyo and Washington agreed on revisions to the 1978 Guidelines for Japan–US Defense Cooperation, the most controversial of which included a description of operations in 'waters surrounding Japan' – understood to include the Taiwan Strait. The US insisted that the guidelines were conceived largely with the Korean Peninsula in mind, while Tokyo explained that the areas in question were not 'being targeted as specific regions', and that the guidelines applied solely to 'situations' arising in areas around Japan. Nonetheless, ARATS chairman Wang pointed out that they would not help to ease China's 'misgivings and worries', and Beijing consistently criticised them.[21] In mid-1997, Seiroku Kajiyama, Japan's chief cabinet secretary, asserted publicly that the guidelines 'naturally cover' Taiwan, for which Tokyo apologised to Beijing.[22] On 22 May 1998, Takano Toshiyuki, director-general of the Foreign Ministry's North American Affairs Bureau, made a similar declaration to the Diet. Although the modernisation of US–Japan security relations was not primarily concerned with Taiwan, stronger ties between the US and Japan would increase the island's security. The relationship between the US, Japan and China inevitably contained an important Taiwanese dimension.

Although the events of 1995–96 drove Japan and the US closer together, both recognised the importance of maintaining workable relations with China. In March 1996, a 'strategic dialogue' began between Liu and Lake. A series of high-level exchanges followed, including Lake's first visit to Beijing in July 1996; a meeting between Clinton and Jiang in Manila in November; Defence Minister Chi's trip to the US in December; and US Vice-President Al Gore's visit to China in April 1997. All paved the way for Jiang's 1997 visit to the US. The joint statement issued on 29 October agreed that a 'sound and stable relationship' would serve the 'fundamental interests' of both sides, but in practice there seemed to be little real basis for strategic cooperation.[23] Both countries spoke of promoting global and regional peace, preventing the proliferation of weapons of mass *the 'three noes'* destruction (WMD), and tackling drug-trafficking and terrorism. In practice, however, these ideas were more aspirational than real. Clinton's return visit between 25 June and 3 July 1998 also produced little of substance, despite lofty talk of 'constructive strategic partnership'. During the visit, 47 bilateral agreements were reached, including a commitment by both sides not to target nuclear weapons at each other, but none was of any strategic significance.

During this period, the US also tried to clarify its position on cross-Strait relations. At a press conference during her visit to China in April 1998, Secretary of State Madeleine Albright made clear that the US:

- did not have a 'one-China, one-Taiwan' or a 'two-China' policy;
- did not support Taiwanese independence; and
- did not support the island's membership in international organisations if statehood was an entry requirement.[24]

Albright added that the US was 'glad when there was dialogue [between China and Taiwan], in terms of trying to get a peaceful resolution to the issue'. Albright's three pledges, which were dubbed the 'three noes', were restated by Susan Shirk, Deputy Assistant Secretary for East Asian and Pacific Affairs, on 20 May, during testimony before the House International Relations Committee. Shirk also repeated Albright's call for cross-Strait dialogue.[25] In response to Clinton's reiteration of the 'three noes' in Shanghai on 30 June 1998, Congress passed a resolution in July affirming the US commitment to Taiwan's security. The House of Representatives also called on Clinton to urge China to renounce the use of force against the island. Critics of the president claimed that, while the US had always maintained a 'one-China' policy, the 'three noes' amounted to adopting China's version of it, thereby representing a significant change in US policy. Taipei argued that the 'three noes' had eroded its bargaining power with Beijing, and was also concerned that other states might follow the US example. However, it became clear during a visit by Jiang to Tokyo in September 1998 that these fears were unjustified, as China failed to persuade Japan to adopt a similar formula.[26]

With or without the 'three noes', there has been no real change in US policy. In a letter to Democratic Senator Robert Torricelli on 18 August 1998, Clinton affirmed 'US support for Taiwan's membership in international organisations that do not require statehood', and stated that the US would 'find appropriate ways for Taiwan's voice to be heard in those that do'. Clinton also reiterated the US commitment to the TRA, and agreed to call on China to renounce the use of force against Taiwan.[27] On 27 August, the US Defense Department announced the planned sale to Taiwan of $350m-worth of missiles and anti-submarine torpedoes.[28]

Sino-American relations were hamstrung not only by the problems of trying to maintain a policy of 'constructive ambiguity' towards Taiwan, but also by the broader attempt to be ambiguous about the nature of the US relationship with China. Despite talk of a 'strategic partnership', relations between the US and China fluctuated wildly following Clinton's visit in 1998. On 11 November, Beijing issued a strong protest in response to the president's meeting with the Dalai Lama in the White House, and US Energy Secretary Bill Richardson's meeting with Lee in Taipei. Beijing demanded that the US should correct its 'mistakes', and charged Washington with violating the terms of Sino-US diplomatic ties.[29] While in Taiwan,

Richardson, the most senior US official to visit the island since 1979, pledged that the US would continue to send envoys despite China's protests.[30] On 12 November, Beijing called in US Ambassador James Sasser for a meeting with Vice-Foreign Minister Yang Jiechi.[31] On the same day, reports emerged that the US suspected China of transferring missile technology to Iran and Pakistan, despite Jiang's pledge in June to strengthen controls on missile exports.[32] The arrest in late 1998 of three pro-democracy activists, and the lengthy sentences they received, further embarrassed the White House, which had continued to speak primarily of its engagement policy with China.

The issue of theatre missile defence (TMD) was a further source of contention between the US and China. On 31 August 1998, North Korea test-launched a three-stage *Taepo-dong* ballistic missile, which overflew Japan. The incident renewed concerns over missile defence for the US and its allies in Asia. On 20 September, the US and *the problem of missiles and TMD* Japan issued a joint statement agreeing to closer cooperation on TMD; four days later, the House of Representatives passed the 1999 National Defense Authorization Bill, which was accompanied by a conference report asking the Department of Defense to study 'the architecture requirements for the establishment and operation of a theater defense system in the Asia-Pacific' in order to protect key regional allies including Japan, Taiwan and South Korea.[33] The bill was passed by the Senate on 1 October.

Beijing's reaction was fierce. On 6 October, the MFA declared its 'deep concern and strong opposition', and denounced clauses in the bill as being 'anti-China'. Beijing warned that, if the bill became law, it would be 'detrimental to the security and stability of Taiwan and the region'.[34] On 11–14 January 1999, US Defense Secretary William Cohen announced in Tokyo that the US would be prepared to help Japan to develop its planned satellite programme, and welcomed Japan's proposal to spend $8m on TMD research and development. The following month, London's *Financial Times* cited a Pentagon report suggesting that Beijing had up to 200 M-9 and M-11 ballistic missiles targeted on Taiwan, which it planned to increase to around 650.[35] Beijing charged that the report was a 'serious intervention in China's internal affairs', and expressed 'serious dissatisfaction and resolute opposition'.[36]

The debate over TMD was of course only part of a broader strategic picture. The perceived threat from China was not the only reason why the US and Japan saw the need for missile defence. Nonetheless, China's fierce reaction to what were still only theoretical proposals, and Beijing's belief that it had a veto over what both Washington and Tokyo saw as defensive measures, only added to concerns about China's long-term intentions. In Beijing on 2 March 1999, Albright acknowledged that ties between the US and China had not lived up to the rhetoric of a 'constructive strategic partnership'.[37]

US domestic politics also made it difficult to improve Sino-American ties. Soon after Albright's visit to China, a House of Representatives committee chaired by Republican Christopher Cox issued a report on Chinese espionage at US research laboratories.[38] The report alleged that China had been stealing US nuclear secrets since the late 1970s, and claimed that enormous damage had been done to US security. Evidence of Chinese spying was, however, ambiguous; a Taiwan-born scientist, Wen Ho Lee, was dismissed from his post at Los Alamos National Laboratory in New Mexico, but no charges were brought against him. Some nuclear experts concluded that there was little truth in the Cox report's key findings.[39] Nonetheless, the outcry was huge. Demands for the resignation of Attorney-General Janet Reno and National Security Advisor Sandy Berger were followed by uproar in the media. Politics, rather than security or science, was the real issue at stake. As has frequently been the case in Sino-US relations, reckless charges were made and China's military capabilities exaggerated; blame was laid at the door of careless policies and actions by the administration. With campaigning for presidential elections in November 2000 under way by mid-1999, there seemed little prospect of any improvement in already battered relations.

Forcing the Issue

While tensions across the Strait persisted, they were far from the crisis atmosphere engendered by Lee's foray to the US, and Beijing's belligerent response. This relative calm was, however, shattered on 9 July 1999, when Lee told a German radio interviewer that, rather than adhering to the 'one-China' policy, relations should be conducted on a 'special state-to-state basis'.[40] Taipei quickly made it clear that, while Lee's remarks surprised observers, they were not a slip of the tongue. On 12 July, Su Chi, the chairman of Taiwan's MAC, confirmed that the government had decided formally to drop the 'one-China' policy; Lee reiterated the new position many times in the months following the interview, while the government worked hard to rally the support of other states, notably the US.[41]

Lee's move may have been intended to improve the chances of the KMT's candidate, Lien Chan, in the 2000 presidential elections (as a two-term incumbent, Lee cannot stand again). Lien, a colourless and stiff campaigner, was lagging behind independent candidate James Soong in opinion polls. (By October 1999, Soong was still the front-runner, with 28% support against 18% for Lien.[42]) Lee may have concluded that the independence *putting relations on a 'special state-to-state basis'* issue would provide a popular platform on which Lien could stand. He may also have reasoned that clarifying the murky stand-off between the two governments in Taiwan's favour would be a historic cap to his tenure. The reiteration by senior US government officials, including Clinton, of the 'three noes'; Washington's refusal to support Taipei's bid for a UN seat; its insistence that no declaration of independence could ever be made; and attempts to improve trade and business relations with China may all have prompted deep concern, causing Lee to change Taipei's position.

Whatever Lee's reasons, his declaration predictably infuriated the Chinese. During July and August, propaganda from Beijing grew shriller, and threats mounted to fold the 'rebel province' back into China, even if that meant using force. China held naval exercises in the South China Sea, flew patrols through the area and paraded large armoured forces through Beijing in a threatening rehearsal for the massive display on 1 October to mark the fiftieth anniversary of the foundation of the PRC. Talk of facing down the US and warnings of the possible beginning of 'World War III' filled the air.[43] At the same time, however, China carefully sounded out the US on its position should conflict break out. Beijing recognised that it was no match for US military power; if anything, the years since 1996 had shown how far behind the Chinese military were.

Washington's initial reaction – encouraging Taiwan to back away from the position that it had adopted – was precisely what

Beijing wanted. Taken by surprise and faced with an unwelcome policy dilemma, the US stated that its position had not changed: there was 'one-China', and it was for China and Taiwan to decide how they would merge at some point in the future. Having delivered this gift to Beijing, however, Washington also reiterated that force should not be used to solve the problem. Senior delegations were sent to Taiwan in an effort to nudge Taipei back to the earlier, shady formulation. When this failed, and Beijing's rhetoric became more intense, the US seemed to feel that it had to remove some of the ambiguity in its own position. On 13 August, Rear-Admiral Timothy Keating, commander of one of the battle groups that had sailed into the Taiwan Strait in 1996, stated that 'China will know if they attempt to undertake any kind of operation – whether it's Taiwan or anything – that they are going to have the US Navy to deal with. We are there in numbers, we're trained, we're ready and we're very powerful'.[44] The dangers of a clash rose dramatically. In mid-August, Lee called for an island-wide missile-defence system, indicating that Taiwan was unwilling to back down.[45] Beijing refused to accept any hint of the existence of an equal state on the island, and the US was forced, by Congress and by its commitments under the TRA, to underwrite Taiwanese security. In the run-up to the March 2000 presidential polls, China eventually decided to cool its rhetoric until the result of the elections had become clear.

Developments in mid-1999 demonstrated that the risks of increased tensions across the Strait, and the real danger of escalation, are ever-present. Civilian and military leaders in Beijing may conclude that any invasion of Taiwan would probably fail, and that other military measures – missile attacks, feints or naval blockades – would have only a limited impact. Nonetheless, Beijing's nationalist agenda makes it difficult for the leadership simply to do nothing in response to actions by Taipei which disrupt the status quo. Unless all the parties concerned accept the existence of a new Taiwan, the dispute between Taiwan and China will remain one of the most contentious and dangerous in East Asia.

conclusion

By the 1980s, China and Taiwan appeared to be putting their long, complex and unpleasant past behind them. By 1995, relations between the two had entered their most serious period of crisis since the late 1950s. As Taiwan's democratisation gathered pace, it became increasingly difficult for the Taiwanese to contemplate reunification with authoritarian China. In turn, as it dawned on China that Taiwan was drifting away, Beijing felt compelled to respond, signalling that it would not tolerate an independent Taiwan. Finally, the vagaries of US domestic politics and Washington's uncertain handling of both countries ensured that its policy was neither clear nor successful. Only at the peak of the crisis did the US show itself willing to defend the status quo.

As soon as the crisis ended, all parties settled back into the incoherence and domestic political complexity that had created it. There has been no real clarification of Taiwan's political order. China's difficult economic-reform process and growing reliance on nationalism to hold an increasingly fractious society together ensure that Beijing will continue to view Taiwanese democracy with deep hostility. US debates over China policy remain as sharp as ever, and the prospects of formulating a coherent position as distant. Only a major reversal of Taiwanese democratisation, or significant progress towards democracy in China, will bring a change for the better in relations across the Strait.

Politics in Taiwan

Taiwan's democracy, although maturing, remains chaotic, and long-term trends are hard to find. While democratisation has opened up the island's politics and society, it remains difficult to determine what the Taiwanese people really want. The military threat from China is still a deep concern, despite economic contacts across the Strait. Beijing has made clear that it will not tolerate independence. Even with political reform on the mainland, no Chinese leader is likely to relinquish the country's claim to Taiwan. As a result, the Taiwanese have sought a lifestyle and an identity that are distinctively theirs, but have drawn back from formal independence.

Under these circumstances, what 'Taiwanese identity' actually means will remain fluid. The increasing strength of Taiwanese consciousness in the 1980s and 1990s had more to do with opposing KMT dominance than denying the population's 'Chineseness'. Just as a Chinese identity does not require belonging to China politically, so too the rise of a Taiwanese identity does not necessarily preclude it. Nonetheless, the political and military threat from China has eroded any remaining identification or affiliation with the mainland. In an MAC opinion poll conducted in August 1999, only 13% of respondents considered themselves Chinese, compared with nearly 50% six years earlier.[1] At the same time, since the late 1980s there has been a significant redistribution of power from mainlanders to native Taiwanese, and ethnicity has become less central in Taiwanese politics. In its place, the concept of the 'New Taiwanese' has gained popular currency. As the political–civic consciousness cultivated by Lee emerges, Taiwanese are developing an increasing sense of nationhood.

Taiwanese remain uncertain about the essence of their new identity

Taiwan's leaders have yet to reach a firm conclusion on the identity question, preferring instead the 'pragmatic diplomacy' that aims to exploit the status quo. Sooner or later, difficult but crucial questions will nonetheless have to be faced. What would Taiwanese prefer, if a choice between independence and unification needed to be made? Will Taiwan's people reject for good being part of a 'greater China', in whatever form? Would Taiwan accept being a small state beside a large, hostile power? In the long term, Taiwan cannot adequately defend itself against China without outside support, but this means relying heavily on the US and Japan. Will the island's search for an independent identity eventually include an independent nuclear deterrent? As the Taiwanese develop a more confident sense of their own identity, these questions will increasingly demand answers.

Chinese and US Attitudes

The tensions of 1999 again demonstrated that the changes under way in Taiwan are the most volatile, and perhaps most important, influence on cross-Strait relations. However, although its behaviour often belies the fact, China too has choices. Beijing's long-standing strategy combines preparations for the day when it might need to use force, efforts to limit Taiwan's international breathing space, and attempts to start political negotiations. This policy is not working, yet China has shown little desire to change it, preferring instead the unimaginative repetition of historical claims of sovereignty as justification for reunification. The 'one country, two systems' model is outdated, particularly given the fact that Hong Kong enjoys far fewer freedoms than Taiwan would demand. Even China's eventual democratisation might not make life easier for Taiwan, since a fragile democracy could be even tougher than the CCP on nationalist issues.

Since 1995, China's military threats against Taiwan have helped to move the island's politics away from extreme positions, and its leaders have tended to couch their demands in terms of a need to be represented in, and identified with, international society. If China relaxed its veto on Taiwan's membership in international organisations, Taiwan's politicians might be encouraged to make concessions of their own, such as establishing the 'three direct links' with the mainland. In addition, by wrong-footing the island's politicians, Beijing may stimulate a more serious debate about what the Taiwanese really want.

US policies too will be inadequate in the long term. 'Strategic ambiguity' alone cannot maintain peace in the Taiwan Strait, and there will again be times when Washington will need to be much clearer about what is acceptable. Nevertheless, the dual nature of US policy has given successive administrations some room for manoeuvre. Denouncing any Chinese attempt to secure reunification by force, while at the same time not endorsing Taiwanese independence, remains an acceptable way to deter Taipei from assuming unconditional US support, and China from behaving recklessly. But ultimately, this ambiguity works only if neither China nor Taiwan is inclined to upset the status quo. As events in 1995–96 and Lee's shift to 'special state-to-state relations' in 1999 showed, Taiwanese domestic politics regularly forces changes. The absence of a coherent US policy towards China since the end of the Cold War has only exacerbated the problem. The pretence that the US has somehow found a 'strategic partnership' with China has inevitably made it more difficult to maintain stability in East Asia.

Pretending that there is 'one-China' will become increasingly difficult for the US as a democratic Taiwan relinquishes its insistence on the principle. By ending the state of civil war with the mainland in 1991, Taiwan reinvented itself as a free, less dogmatic actor. Lee's declaration in 1999 was merely another reminder that there is a new Taiwan, and that a peaceful settlement to the dispute across the Strait cannot now be built on the basis of 'one-China'. While this is well-understood in the US and other democracies, 'one-China, one-Taiwan' is diplomatically inconvenient, possibly even dangerous. In the absence of a major crisis in the Strait, there is no evidence that the outside world will accept the new Taiwan, and recognise the right of the Taiwanese people to choose their future. But in the end, diplomacy that does not match the reality of a new Taiwan is likely to lead to fresh crises.

appendix

Extracts from Key Documents

Joint Communiqué of the United States of America and the People's Republic of China, 28 February 1972

Paragraph Eight

There are essential differences between China and the United States in their social systems and foreign policies. However, the two sides agreed that countries, regardless of their social systems, should conduct their relations on the principles of respect for the sovereignty and territorial integrity of all states, non-aggression against other states, non-interference in the internal affairs of other states, equality and mutual benefit, and peaceful coexistence. International disputes should be settled on this basis, without resorting to the use or threat of force. The United States and the People's Republic of China are prepared to apply these principles to their mutual relations.

Paragraph Nine

With these principles of international relations in mind the two sides stated that:

- progress toward the normalization of relations between China and the United States is in the interests of all countries
- both wish to reduce the danger of international military conflict
- neither should seek hegemony in the Asia-Pacific region and

each is opposed to efforts by any other country or group of countries to establish such hegemony

• neither is prepared to negotiate on behalf of any third party or to enter into agreements or understandings with the other directed at other states.

Paragraph Eleven

The two sides reviewed the long-standing serious disputes between China and the United States. The Chinese side reaffirmed its position: the Taiwan question is the crucial question obstructing the normalization of relations between China and the United States; the Government of the People's Republic of China is the sole legal government of China; Taiwan is a province of China which has long been returned to the motherland; the liberation of Taiwan is China's internal affair in which no other country has the right to interfere; and all US forces and military installations must be withdrawn from Taiwan. The Chinese Government firmly opposes any activities which aim at the creation of 'one China, one Taiwan', 'one China, two governments', 'two Chinas', an 'independent Taiwan' or advocate that 'the status of Taiwan remains to be determined'.

Paragraph Twelve

The US side declared: The United States acknowledges that all Chinese on either side of the Taiwan Strait maintain there is but one China and that Taiwan is a part of China. The United States Government does not challenge that position. It reaffirms its interest in a peaceful settlement of the Taiwan question by the Chinese themselves. With this prospect in mind, it affirms the ultimate objective of the withdrawal of all US forces and military installations from Taiwan. In the meantime, it will progressively reduce its forces and military installations on Taiwan as the tension in the area diminishes. The two sides agreed that it is desirable to broaden the understanding between the two peoples. To this end, they discussed specific areas in such fields as science, technology, culture, sports and journalism, in which people-to-people contacts and exchanges would be mutually beneficial. Each side undertakes to facilitate the further development of such contacts and exchanges.

Joint Communiqué of the United States of America and the People's Republic of China, 1 January 1979

1. The United States of America and the People's Republic of China have agreed to recognize each other and to establish diplomatic relations as of January 1, 1979.

2. The United States of America recognizes the Government of the People's Republic of China as the sole legal Government of China. Within this context, the people of the United States will maintain cultural, commercial, and other unofficial relations with the people of Taiwan.

3. The United States of America and the People's Republic of China reaffirm the principles agreed on by the two sides in the Shanghai Communiqué and emphasize once again that:

4. Both wish to reduce the danger of international military conflict.

5. Neither should seek hegemony in the Asia-Pacific region or in any other region of the world and each is opposed to efforts by any other country or group of countries to establish such hegemony.

6. Neither is prepared to negotiate on behalf of any third party or to enter into agreements or understandings with the other directed at other states.

7. The Government of the United States of America acknowledges the Chinese position that there is but one China and Taiwan is part of China.

8. Both believe that normalization of Sino-American relations is not only in the interest of the Chinese and American peoples but also contributes to the cause of peace in Asia and the world.

The United States of America and the People's Republic of China will exchange Ambassadors and establish Embassies on March 1, 1979.

The Taiwan Relations Act, 10 April 1979

Section 2 (a)

The President having terminated governmental relations between the United States and the governing authorities on Taiwan recognized by the United States as the Republic of China prior to January 1, 1979, the Congress finds that the enactment of this Act is necessary:

(1) to help maintain peace, security, and stability in the Western Pacific; and
(2) to promote the foreign policy of the United States by authorizing the continuation of commercial, cultural, and other relations between the people of the United States and the people on Taiwan.

Section 2 (b)

It is the policy of the United States:

(1) to preserve and promote extensive, close, and friendly commercial, cultural, and other relations between the people of the United States and the people on Taiwan, as well as the people on the China mainland and all other peoples of the Western Pacific area;
(2) to declare that peace and stability in the area are in the political, security, and economic interests of the United States, and are matters of international concern;
(3) to make clear that the United States decision to establish diplomatic relations with the People's Republic of China rests upon the expectation that the future of Taiwan will be determined by peaceful means;
(4) to consider any effort to determine the future of Taiwan by other than peaceful means, including by boycotts or embargoes, a threat to the peace and security of the Western Pacific area and of grave concern to the United States;
(5) to provide Taiwan with arms of a defensive character; and
(6) to maintain the capacity of the United States to resist any resort to force or other forms of coercion that would

jeopardize the security, or the social or economic system, of the people on Taiwan.

Section 2 (c)

Nothing contained in this Act shall contravene the interest of the United States in human rights, especially with respect to the human rights of all the approximately eighteen million inhabitants of Taiwan. The preservation and enhancement of the human rights of all the people on Taiwan are hereby reaffirmed as objectives of the United States.

Section 3 (a)

In furtherance of the policy set forth in Section 2 of this Act, the United States will make available to Taiwan such defense articles and defense services in such quantity as may be necessary to enable Taiwan to maintain a sufficient self-defense capability.

Section 3 (b)

The President and the Congress shall determine the nature and quantity of such defense articles and services based solely upon their judgment of the needs of Taiwan, in accordance with procedures established by law. Such determination of Taiwan's defense needs shall include review by United States military authorities in connection with recommendations to the President and the Congress.

Section 3 (c)

The President is directed to inform the Congress promptly of any threat to the security or the social or economic system of the people on Taiwan and any danger to the interests of the United States arising therefrom. The President and the Congress shall determine, in accordance with constitutional processes, appropriate action by the United States in response to any such danger.

The Nine-Point Proposal, 30 September 1981

1. In order to bring an end to the unfortunate separation of the Chinese nation as early as possible, we propose that the Communist Party and the Kuomintang Party hold talks on a reciprocal basis, to cooperate for the third time to accomplish the great cause of national reunification.

2. We propose that the two sides of the [Taiwan] Strait make arrangements to facilitate reunions and visits by relatives and tourists as well as academic, cultural and sports exchanges, and reach an agreement thereupon.

3. After the country is reunified, Taiwan can enjoy a high degree of autonomy as a special administrative region (SAR) and it can retain its armed forces. The Central Government will not interfere with local affairs on Taiwan.

4. Taiwan's current socioeconomic system will remain unchanged, as will its way of life and its economic and cultural relations with foreign countries. There will be no encroachment on the proprietary rights and lawful right of inheritance over private property, houses, land and enterprises, or on foreign investments.

5. People in authority and representative personages of various circles in Taiwan may take posts of leadership in national political bodies and participate in running the state.

6. When Taiwan's local finance is in difficulty, the Central Government may subsidize it as is fit for the circumstances.

7. Taiwan Chinese who wish to come and settle on the mainland will be guaranteed that proper arrangements will be made for them, that there will be no discrimination against them, and that they will have freedom of entry and exit.

8. Taiwan's industrialists and businesses are welcome to invest and engage in various economic undertakings on the mainland, and their legal rights, interests and profits are guaranteed.

9. The reunification of the motherland is the responsibility of all Chinese. We sincerely welcome Taiwan Chinese of all circles to make proposals and suggestions regarding affairs of state through various channels and in various ways.

Joint Communiqué of the United States of America and the People's Republic of China, 17 August 1982

1. In the Joint Communiqué on the Establishment of Diplomatic Relations on January 1, 1979, issued by the Government of the United States of America and the People's Republic of China, the United States of America recognized the Government of the People's Republic of China as the sole legal Government of China, and it acknowledged the Chinese position that there is but one China and Taiwan is part of China. Within that context, the two sides agreed that the people of the United States would continue to maintain cultural, commercial, and other unofficial relations with the people of Taiwan. On this basis, relations between the United States and China were normalized.

2. The question of United States arms sales to Taiwan was not settled in the course of negotiations between the two countries on establishing diplomatic relations. The two sides held differing positions, and the Chinese side stated that it would raise the issue again following normalization. Recognizing that this issue would seriously hamper the development of United States–China relations, they have held further discussions on it, during and since the meetings between President Ronald Reagan and Premier Zhao Ziyang and between Secretary of State Alexander M. Haig, Jr. and Vice Premier and Foreign Minister Huang Hua in October 1981.

3. Respect for each other's sovereignty and territorial integrity and non-interference in each other's internal affairs constitute the fundamental principles guiding United States–China relations. These principles were confirmed in the Shanghai Communiqué of February 28, 1972 and reaffirmed in the Joint Communiqué on the Establishment of Diplomatic Relations which came into effect on

January 1, 1979. Both sides emphatically state that these principles continue to govern all aspects of their relations.

4. The Chinese Government reiterates that the question of Taiwan is China's internal affair. The Message to Compatriots in Taiwan issued by China on January 1, 1979 promulgated a fundamental policy of striving for peaceful reunification of the motherland. The Nine-Point Proposal put forward by China on September 30, 1981 represented a further major effort under this fundamental policy to strive for a peaceful solution to the Taiwan question.

5. The United States Government attaches great importance to its relations with China, and reiterates that it has no intention of infringing on Chinese sovereignty and territorial integrity, or interfering in China's internal affairs, or pursuing a policy of 'two Chinas' or 'one China, one Taiwan'. The United States Government understands and appreciates the Chinese policy of striving for a peaceful resolution of the Taiwan question as indicated in China's Message to Compatriots in Taiwan issued on January 1, 1979 and the Nine-Point Proposal put forward by China on September 30, 1981. The new situation which has emerged with regard to the Taiwan question also provides favorable conditions for the settlement of United States–China differences over United States arms sales to Taiwan.

Having in mind the foregoing statements of both sides, the United States Government states that it does not seek to carry out a long-term policy of arms sales to Taiwan, that its arms sales to Taiwan will not exceed, either in qualitative or in quantitative terms, the level of those supplied in recent years since the establishment of diplomatic relations between the United States and China, and that it intends gradually to reduce its sale of arms to Taiwan, leading, over a period of time, to a final resolution. In so stating, the United States acknowledges China's consistent position regarding the thorough settlement of this issue.

6. In order to bring about, over a period of time, a final settlement of the question of United States arms sales to Taiwan, which is an issue

rooted in history, the two Governments will make every effort to adopt measures and create conditions conducive to the thorough settlement of this issue.

7. The development of United States–China relations is not only in the interests of the two peoples but also conducive to peace and stability in the world. The two sides are determined, on the principle of equality and mutual benefit, to strengthen their ties in the economic, cultural, educational, scientific, technological and other fields and make strong, joint efforts for the continued development of relations between the Governments and peoples of the United States and China.

8. In order to bring about the healthy development of United States–China relations, maintain world peace and oppose aggression and expansion, the two Governments reaffirm the principles agreed on by the two sides in the Shanghai Communiqué and the Joint Communiqué on the Establishment of Diplomatic Relations. The two sides will maintain contact and hold appropriate consultations on bilateral and international issues of common interest.

Chapter 1

[1] Western ethnologists agree with their Japanese colleagues. The Chinese theory is premised on the discovery in Guizhou early in the twentieth century of an aboriginal tribe which worshipped the image of a dog as its founder. This echoes a Taiyal myth, according to which the tribe was born out of sex between a dog and a princess. See Simon Long, *Taiwan: China's Last Frontier* (London: Macmillan, 1991), pp. 3–4.

[2] See, for example, John King Fairbank, *The Chinese World Order: Traditional China's Foreign Relations* (Cambridge, MA: Harvard University Press, 1968).

[3] Long, *Taiwan*, chapter 1.

[4] Gary Klintworth, *New China, New Taiwan: Taiwan's Changing Role in the Asia-Pacific Region* (New York: Longman, 1995), p. 33.

[5] *Ibid.*, chapter 2.

[6] Christopher Hughes, *Taiwan and Chinese Nationalism* (London: Routledge, 1997).

[7] Gordon Chang, *Friends and Enemies: The United States, China and the Soviet Union, 1948–1972* (Stanford, CA: Stanford University Press, 1990).

[8] June Dreyer, 'A History of Cross-Strait Exchange', in James R. Lilley and Chuck Downs (eds), *Crisis in the Taiwan Strait* (Washington DC: National Defense University Press, 1997), p. 23.

[9] Author interviews, Taipei, July 1998.

[10] Jean-Pierre Cabestan, 'Taiwan's Mainland Policy: Normalisation, Yes; Reunification, No', *China Quarterly*, no. 148, December 1996, p. 1,266.

[11] *Ibid.*, p 1,268.

[12] See *International Financial Statistics Yearbook, 1992* (Washington DC: International Monetary Fund, 1992), pp. 108–15.

[13] Chi Schive, *Taiwan's Economic Role in East Asia* (Washington DC: Center for Strategic and International Studies (CSIS), 1995), p. 26.

[14] There was substantial *de facto* 'direct' trade between China and Taiwan, in the form of

transhipment and illegal direct shipment, especially amongst medium and small Taiwanese businesses. See Sung Yun-wing, 'Economic Interdependence in the Natural Economic Territories', in Jane Khanna (ed.), *Southern China, Hong Kong and Taiwan: Evolution of a Subregional Economy* (Washington DC: CSIS, 1995), pp. 28–29.
[15] See Yun-han Chu, 'The ABCs of Cross-Strait Policy', The Republic of China on Taiwan Western Europe Website, March 1997, www.roc-taiwan.org.uk/info/fcr97/5/p42.htm.

Chapter 2

[1] Hughes, *Taiwan and Chinese Nationalism*, p. 27.
[2] Hung-mao Tien, 'Elections and Taiwan's Development', in Hung-mao Tien (ed.), *Taiwan's Electoral Politics and Democratic Transition: Riding the Third Wave* (New York: East Gate, 1996), p. 10.
[3] Hughes, *Taiwan and Chinese Nationalism*, p. 51.
[4] *Ibid.*, p. 41.
[5] Long, *Taiwan*, p. 194.
[6] Yun-han Chu and Tse-min Lin, 'The Process of Democratic Consolidation in Taiwan: Social Cleavage, Electoral Competition, and the Emerging Party System', in Tien (ed.), *Taiwan's Electoral Politics*, p. 83.
[7] *Ibid.*, p. 85.
[8] *Ibid.*, p. 84.
[9] *Ibid.*
[10] See Lien Chan, 'The ROCOT Belongs in the UN', *Orbis*, vol. 37, no. 4, Autumn 1993, p. 635.
[11] Hung-mao Tien, 'Taiwan in 1995: Electoral Politics and Cross-Strait Relations', *Asian Survey*, vol. 36, no. 1, January 1996, p. 63.

[12] Michael Yahuda, 'The International Standing of the Republic of China on Taiwan', *China Quarterly*, no. 148, December 1996, p. 1,332.
[13] See 'The Republic of China on Taiwan and the United Nations', Ministry of Foreign Affairs, Republic of China, August 1995.
[14] John W. Garver, *Face Off: China, the United States, and Taiwan's Democratisation* (Seattle, WA and London: University of Washington Press, 1997), p. 31.
[15] Yahuda, 'The International Standing of the Republic of China on Taiwan', p. 1,337.
[16] Author interview with former US Assistant Secretary of State Winston Lord, Washington DC, 3 July 1998.
[17] Author interviews, Taipei, Beijing and Washington DC, July–August 1998.
[18] Michael Ying-Mao Kau, 'The Power Structure in Taiwan's Political Economy', *Asian Survey*, vol. 36, no. 3, March 1996, p. 299.
[19] *Ibid.*, p. 299.
[20] *Ibid.*, pp. 299–300.
[21] *Ibid.*, p. 303.
[22] Garver, *Face Off*, p. 90.

Chapter 3

[1] See Harry Harding, *A Fragile Relationship: The United States and China since 1972* (Washington DC: Brookings Institution, 1992), p. 225–26.
[2] This discussion of Beijing's perceptions is drawn from author interviews with officials, academics, and think-tank personnel in Beijing, Shanghai, Xiamen, Taipei, Singapore, Washington DC and New York, July–August 1998.

[3] Robert Sutter, *China's Changing Conditions*, CRS Issue Brief 93114 (Washington DC: Congressional Research Service, December 1996).
[4] 'Conditions for Renewal of Most Favored Nation Status for The People's Republic of China in 1994', Executive Order 12850, www.pub.whitehouse.gov.
[5] US Department of Defense, *United States Security Strategy for the East Asia-Pacific Region* (Washington DC: Department of Defense, February 1995), pp. i, 15.
[6] 'Joint Communiqué of the United States of America and the People's Republic of China, August 17, 1982', United States Information Agency (USIA), www.usia.gov/regional/ea/uschina/jtcomm2.htm.
[7] 'Adjustments to US Policy Toward Taiwan Explained', Transcript of a Background Briefing at the State Department, Washington DC, 9 September 1994.
[8] The clause allowing officials to transit the US was inserted only after persistent Taiwanese lobbying. Author interviews, Washington DC, Beijing and Taipei, June–July 1998.
[9] Greg Austin, 'Taiwan and Chinese Military Power in Japan's Domestic Politics', in Greg Austin (ed.), *Missile Diplomacy and Taiwan's Future: Innovations in Politics and Military Power*, Canberra Paper on Strategy and Defence 122, (Canberra: Australian National University, 1997), p. 92.
[10] Yahuda, 'The International Standing of the Republic of China on Taiwan', p. 1,334.
[11] Author interviews, Beijing, Shanghai and Xiamen, August 1998.
[12] Garver, *Face Off*, p. 25.
[13] *Ibid*.
[14] *Ibid*.
[15] Author interviews, Beijing, Shanghai and Taipei, July 1998.
[16] Yahuda, 'The International Standing of the Republic of China on Taiwan'.
[17] Jiang Zemin, 'Continue to Promote the Reunification of the Motherland', *Xinhua News Agency*, 30 January 1995.

Chapter 4

[1] Garver, *Face Off*, p. 69.
[2] See Barton Gellman, 'Reappraisal Led to New China Policy', *Washington Post*, 22 June 1998, p. A1.
[3] Garver, *Face Off*, pp. 69–70.
[4] *Xinhua News Agency*, 23 May 1995, in Foreign Broadcast Information Service (FBIS), *Daily Report*, 23 May 1995, pp. 3–5, cited in Garver, *Face Off*, p. 72.
[5] Garver, *Face Off*, p. 72.
[6] Author interview with State Department official, Washington DC, July 1998.
[7] Author interviews, Washington DC, July 1998.
[8] Joanne Jaw-ling Chang, *1995–1996 Taihai Weiji: Huafu, Bejing, Taipei Zhi Juetse Xiwu Janto* (Taipei: Academia Sinica, 1998), pp. 99–143.
[9] Author interviews, Washington DC, July 1998.
[10] 'ROC Put Off Military Drill to Ease Tensions in Taiwan Straits', *Free China Journal*, 12 April 1996, www.publish.gio.gov.tw.
[11] 'China Accuses US of Escalating', *New York Times*, 11 March 1996.
[12] Author interviews, Washington DC, July 1998.
[13] Author interviews, Washington DC, July 1998.
[14] Winston Lord, 'US Policy towards China: Security and Military

Considerations', Statement before the Subcommittee on East Asian and Pacific Affairs of the Senate Foreign Relations Committee, Washington DC, 11 October 1995.

[15] US Secretary of State Warren Christopher, comments at a press conference prior to an Association of South-East Asian Nations (ASEAN) meeting, Brunei, 1 August 1995.

[16] See Robert Sutter, *China Policy: Crisis over Taiwan, 1995 – A Post-Mortem*, CRS Report for Congress 95-1173 F, 5 December 1995.

[17] Author interviews, Beijing and Shanghai, July 1998.

[18] Author interviews with officials present at the meeting, Washington DC, July 1998.

[19] Press briefing by Assistant Secretary of State for East Asia Winston Lord and Director of Asian Affairs Robert Suettinger, New York, 24 October 1995.

[20] Garver, *Face Off*, p. 86.

[21] Author interviews, Washington DC, July 1998.

[22] Author interview with officials from the Pentagon, State Department and White House, Washington DC, June–July 1998.

[23] Garver, *Face Off*, p. 96.

[24] US Assistant Secretary of Defense Joseph Nye, remarks at the Asia Society, Seattle, WA, 12 December 1995.

[25] Garver, *Face Off*, p. 97.

[26] *Chinese Exercise 'Strait 961': 8–25 March 1996* (Washington DC: Office of Naval Intelligence, 1996), p. 7.

[27] Gellman, 'Reappraisal Led to New China Policy'; and author interviews, Washington DC, July 1998.

[28] Gellman, 'Reappraisal Led to New China Policy'.

[29] Winston Lord, 'The United States and the Security of Taiwan', and

Kurt Campbell, 'Statement before the Sub-committee on East Asia and the Pacific, Senate Foreign Relations Committee', Washington DC, 7 February 1996.

[30] Garver, *Face Off*, p. 99.

[31] Sutter, *Taiwan: US Policy Choices*.

[32] *Chinese Exercise 'Strait 961'*, p. 1.

[33] Gellman, 'Reappraisal Led to New China Policy'; and author interviews, Washington DC, July 1998.

[34] 'Viewing PLA Exercises in Fujian – Strong Military Pressure Will Be Maintained from Western Shore of Taiwan Strait', *Wen Wei Po*, 22 March 1996.

[35] Author interview with officials from the Pentagon, State Department and White House, Washington DC, June–July 1998; and Garver, *Face Off*, pp. 101–2.

[36] Gellman, 'Reappraisal Led to New China Policy'; and author interviews, Washington DC, July 1998.

[37] US Secretary of Defense William Perry, 'Department of Defense News Briefing', 8 March 1996, www.defenselink.mil/news/ Mar1996/t030896_t0308hon.html.

[38] See Gary Klintworth, 'Lessons Learnt', in Austin (ed.), *Missile Diplomacy and Taiwan's Future*, p. 253.

[39] *Ibid.*; Gellman, 'Reappraisal Led to New China Policy'; and author interviews, Washington DC, July 1998.

[40] Captain Michael Doubleday, 'Department of Defense News Briefing', 12 March 1996, www.defenselink.mil/news/ Mar1996/t031296_t0312asd.html

[41] Garver, *Face Off*, p. 107; and Geoffrey Crothall, 'Li Warns US against Show of Force in Strait', *South China Morning Post*, 18 March 1996, p. 1.

Chapter 5

[1] 'Taiwanese President Calls for New Era', *Time Daily*, 20 May 1996, www.pathfinder.com/time/daily/0,2960,6683,00.html.

[2] President Lee Teng-hui, quoted in Julian Baum, 'Wishful Thinking: Taiwan Rejects China's Grand Design for Reunification', *Far Eastern Economic Review*, 17 July 1997.

[3] Keith B. Richburg, 'Leader Asserts Taiwan Is Independent, Sovereign', *Washington Post*, 8 November 1997, p. A01.

[4] 'Cross-Strait Tourism and Trade Rise', *Hong Kong Standard*, 17 October 1997.

[5] Mainland Affairs Council (MAC), 'Preliminary Statistics of Cross-Strait Economic Relations', 19 August 1999, www.mac.gov.tw.

[6] Baum, 'Wishful Thinking'.

[7] 'How the Missiles Help California', *Time Daily*, 1 April 1996, www.pathfinder.com/time/magazine/archive/1996/dom/960401/boom.html.

[8] Hsu Hsin-liang, 'Party Must Represent Mainstream', speech to a press conference, Taipei, 7 January 1997, www.taiwandc.org/dpp/19603.htm.

[9] 'Taiwan's Milestone', *Washington Post*, 17 December 1997, p. A24; and 'Taiwan Shows the Way', *International Herald Tribune*, 18 December 1997, p. 8.

[10] 'Opposition DPP Chief Rules Out Plebiscite on Independence', *Taiwan Central News Agency*, in *BBC Summary of World Broadcasts, The Far East* (SWB/FE) D3099/F, 11 December 1997.

[11] Democratic Progressive Party, 'Opinion Poll on Party Image', 28 October 1998, www.dpp.org.tw/a/6-03.html.

[12] 'Election Results Offer Rebirth for Taiwan's Nationalists', *Associated Press*, 6 December 1998.

[13] '"Expert" Urges Political Focus in Cross-Strait Talks', *Wen Wei Po*, 14 December 1997, in SWB/FE D3101/F, 16 December 1997.

[14] 'Stand Firm on Taiwan', *Asian Wall Street Journal*, 20–21 February 1998.

[15] Jason Blatt, 'Ex-Clinton Aide Urges Minor Issues Action', *South China Morning Post*, 6 March 1998.

[16] 'Koo's Trip Will Be an "Exchange"', *China News*, 26 July 1998.

[17] Lawrence Chung, 'Taiwan Says No Change in Bottom Line on China', *Reuters*, 2 November 1998.

[18] 'Taiwan Calls for Closer Ties', *Associated Press*, 2 November 1998.

[19] *Ibid.*

[20] *US–Japan Joint Declaration on Security: Alliance for the Twenty-First Century*, 17 April 1996, www.state.gov/regions/eap/japan/jointsec.html.

[21] 'Taiwan Policy Chief Urges Japan to Reduce "Obscurity" of Japanese–US Defence Guidelines', *Xinhua News Agency Domestic Service*, Beijing, 20 January 1998, in SWB/FE D3132/G, 23 January 1998.

[22] Nicholas Kristof, 'Japan Agonizes over Its Role in Event of Conflict over Taiwan', *New York Times*, 25 August 1997.

[23] 'Joint US–China Statement, October 29, 1997', US Department of State, www.usia.gov/regional/ea/uschina/joint29.htm.

[24] Secretary of State Madeleine K. Albright, remarks at a press conference, Beijing, 30 April 1998, www.secretary.state.gov www/statements/1998/980430b.html.

[25] 'Relations with China, Taiwan not a Zero-Sum Game', Testimony by

Deputy Assistant Secretary of State for East Asian and Pacific Affairs Susan L. Shirk before the House International Relations Committee, Washington DC, 20 May 1998, www.state.gov/www/policy_remarks/1998/980520_shirk_taiwan.html.

26 'Japan Reluctant to State "Three No's" Policy against Taiwan', *Agence France-Presse*, 19 August 1998.

27 'Clinton Reaffirms Commitment to Taiwan', *Central News Agency*, 26 August 1998.

28 Benjamin Kang Lim, 'China Denounces US Missile Sale to Taiwan', *Reuters*, 27 August 1998.

29 Christian Virant, 'China Hits Out at US over Taiwan, Tibet', *ibid.*, 11 November 1998.

30 Lawrence Chung, 'Richardson Says US Will Send More Envoys to Taiwan', *ibid.*, 11 November 1998.

31 Christian Virant, 'China Calls in US Envoy over Taiwan, Dalai Lama', *ibid.*, 12 November 1998.

32 Charles Hutzler, 'China May Have Moved Missile Data', *Associated Press*, 12 November 1998.

33 'Taiwan Welcomes US House Demand for TMD Coverage for Taiwan', *Central News Agency*, 25 September 1998.

34 'Beijing Slams as "Anti-China" US–Japan Plan for Missile Defense in Asia', *Agence France-Presse*, 6 October 1998.

35 Tony Walker and Stephen Fidler, 'China: Taiwan Missiles Build Up', *Financial Times*, 10 February 1999, p. 1.

36 'Beijing Blasts Washington over Pentagon Missile Report', *Reuters*, 1 March 1999.

37 James Kynge, 'Albright Braves Visit', *Financial Times*, 3 March 1999, p. 4.

38 *US National Security and Military/ Commercial Concerns with the People's Republic of China*, US House of Representatives Select Committee, March 1999, hillsource.house.gov/CoxReport/report.

39 Lars Erik Nelson, 'Washington: The Yellow Peril', *New York Review of Books*, 15 July 1999, pp. 6–9.

40 'Interview with *Deutsche Welle*', Information Division, Taipei Economic and Cultural Office, New York, 12 July 1999, www.cultural-division.org/current/lee712.htm.

41 'Tapei Rebuts Beijing's "One-China" Principle', *MAC News Briefing*, 12 July 1999, http://www.mac.gov.tw/english.

42 'James Soong Still Leads in Poll', *Central News Agency*, 3 October 1999.

43 See Gerald Segal, 'War Prospects in Asia Are Both Remote and Scary', *International Herald Tribune*, 24 August 1999, p. 6.

44 Jonathan S. Landay, 'In Tense Asia, US Juggles Carrots and Sticks', *Christian Science Monitor*, 18 August 1999, p. 2; and Russell Flannery, 'Taiwan Trumpets Presence of US Navy Ships', *Wall Street Journal*, 13 August 1999, p. 8.

45 'Taiwan Leader Seeks Missile Defense', *Associated Press*, 19 August 1999.

Conclusion

1 MAC, 'The New Taiwanese: Ethnic Identity of People in Taiwan', August 1999, www.mac.gov.tw/english/pos/880818/nt8808.htm.

DATE DUE

GAYLORD			PRINTED IN U.S.A.